POCKET
Factfile
of
MAMMALS

Lowe & B. Hould
Publishers

Text and Maps: Jill Bailey

Project Editor: Graham Bateman
Designer: Frankie Wood
Cartographic Manager: Richard Watts
Proof Readers: Lin Thomas,
                 Marian Dreier
Production: Clive Sparling

Planned and produced by
Andromeda Oxford Ltd
11–15 The Vineyard
Abingdon
Oxfordshire OX14 3PX

Published by Borders Press,
a division of Borders, Inc.
311 Maynard, Ann Arbor,
Michigan, 48104.

Lowe & B. Hould, Publishers is a
trademark of Borders Properties, Inc.

ISBN 0–681–21995–5

Origination by H.B.M. Print Ltd,
Singapore

Maps produced by Cosmographics,
England

Printed by Tien Wah Press, Singapore

CONTENTS

INTRODUCTION

Mammals represent the pinnacle of evolution; they are the most advanced forms of life yet to appear on this planet. They range from the largest animal ever to have lived, the Blue whale (p. 48), to the tiny Kitti's hognosed bat (p. 171), 100 million times smaller. Mammals have diversified to fill every kind of habitat: Polar bears (p. 18) and reindeer (p. 99) inhabit the Arctic wastes, while camels (pp. 94, 95) can survive in deserts without water for long periods; many monkeys (pp. 63–75) spend almost their entire lives above ground high in the trees, while moles (p. 163) and gophers (p. 132) seldom leave their underground tunnels, and the whales and dolphins (pp. 36–50) live mainly in the sea, a few in fresh water.

All mammals share certain features. They have an internal skeleton of bones linked together by flexible joints. Their bodies are covered in hair (sometimes very sparsely) and they secrete milk to feed their young. Hair traps a layer of air next to the skin, which insulates it from extremes of temperature around it, helping the mammal to control its body temperature. Mammals also sweat, losing heat as the sweat evaporates. Mammals have a variety of shapes and sizes of teeth, adapted to their different diets.

Despite all these common features, mammals are a very varied group of animals. The wide range of body forms reflects a diversity of lifestyles. Fast-moving predators like the cheetah (p. 8) are slender, muscular and long-legged, while underwater hunters such as Bottle-nosed dolphins (p. 38) are sleek and streamlined, with paddles instead of legs. Hamsters (p. 144) and marmots (p. 131), which need to store food as fat to survive harsh winters, may become very fat as winter approaches. Besides running and swimming, other forms of locomotion have been adopted: kangaroos and wallabies (p. 200–205) cover the ground rapidly in huge leaps, while bats (pp. 170–177) have evolved flight, and various squirrels (p. 127) have acquired the ability to glide long distances through the air.

The mammals arose about 200 million years ago, when dinosaurs still roamed the Earth. Since then, they have adapted to many changing environments. Today there are mammals to exploit almost every situation, from clearing up carcasses, to exploiting the flowers and fruits of the forest, and feasting on the wastes of human habitation. Some mammals, such as the nectar-feeding bats (p. 177) and the bamboo-eating Giant panda (p. 24), are extreme specialists while others, like the raccoon (p. 23) and Red fox (p. 16), are expert scavengers. With the spread of human settlements across the globe, some mammals, such as the House mouse (p. 138), have thrived, taking advantage of new foods in the form of crops and garbage, while others have been unable to survive the destruction of their natural habitats and have vanished for ever, for example, the Tasmanian wolf (p. 187).

About This Book

This book is a handy, pocket-sized overview of the wide range of mammals that live in various parts of the world. Most of the major groups of mammals are represented and examples are taken from all parts of the world. Here you will find the common and the rare, the normal and the weird. **Color artwork** gives a clear picture of the appearance of the animals and sometimes indicates a characteristic type of behavior. A **distribution map** shows in which parts of the world each species is found. Land distribution is shown in green and that in seas and oceans in dark blue; where the distribution is very restricted a square has been placed over the area in question. The **text** presents important information about the kind of habitat the animal lives in and its global distribution, its size, form and diet, its breeding behavior, its conservation status, as well as other facts of interest. On the rare occasion where statistics are missing, this is because they are not known for certain.

Here we have grouped together similar types of mammal (often related families) for quick reference. The *Carnivores* are mammals that mostly live by killing other animals; they usually have specialized teeth for gripping struggling prey and dealing with flesh and bones. *Sea Mammals* spend their entire lives in the oceans and seas; they have streamlined, torpedo-shaped bodies, with limbs modified to form paddles. The *Primates* are the monkey-like mammals; they have well-developed brains, and eyes that face forward for accurate judgment of distances – an adaptation to living in trees. The *Large Herbivores* are chiefly hoofed mammals that feed mainly on plants; quite often they live in large herds. *Small Mammals* is a group of mainly small mammals not found in the other groups. It includes squirrels, mice, rats and other rodents; rabbits and hares; insect-eating mammals such as hedgehogs, shrews and moles; anteaters; and the bats. *Monotremes and Marsupials* are two unique groups, most of which, but not all, come from Australia and have evolved to fill all the niches typical of animals elsewhere in the world.

Abbreviations

HB head-body length   TL tail length   SH shoulder height   WT weight

LION

Panthera leo

Family: Felidae

LIONS RELY ON STEALTH AND CUNNING *to stalk their prey. Lionesses work together to make the kill; pride males rarely hunt.*

DISTRIBUTION: originally from Africa, Arabia and the Balkans to India; now confined to the African grasslands and open woodlands south of the southern Sahara, and (the Asian subspecies) the Gir sanctuary in northwest India.

SIZE: HB 1.4–2.5 m (5–8.2 ft); TL 0.7–1.0 m (2.3–3.3 ft); SH 0.8–1.1 m (2.6–3.6 ft); WT 120–350 kg (265–772 lb); males larger than females.

FORM: coat light tawny, white on belly and inner legs; backs of ears black; mane of male ranges from tawny to black; the young have a rosette pattern.

DIET: hoofed mammals, such as antelopes, gazelles, zebras, giraffes and wild hogs, and the young of larger mammals like elephants and rhinos.

BREEDING: 2–4 cubs born at any time of year after a gestation of 100–119 days; cubs are not completely independent of their mothers until about two and a half years of age.

OTHER INFORMATION: live in small family groups called prides, in which the females are usually related. Lifespan 12–15 years in the wild, up to 30 in captivity.

CONSERVATION STATUS: not seriously threatened, but numbers are declining as a result of habitat loss.

TIGER

Panthera tigris

Family: Felidae

DISTRIBUTION: originally North China to India and Southeast Asia, and around Caspian Sea. Now isolated and very rare. It lives in a varied habitat, but requires dense cover of vegetation.

SIZE: varies with subspecies. Indian (male) HB 2.7–3 m (8.8–10.2 ft); SH 91 cm (3 ft); WT 180–260 kg (396–570 lb). Largest recorded (Siberian male), WT 384 kg (845 lb).

FORM: coat, stripes of black/dark brown over lighter sandy-brown background; white patches on face and underparts.

DIET: a specialized stalk and ambush hunter of large mammals.

ONCE RELATIVELY COMMON IN TROPICAL ASIA, TIGERS *are in desperate plight, with three subspecies probably extinct in China, Bali and the Caspian Sea area. Loss of habitat is due to human encroachment.*

BREEDING: either seasonal (winter mating in north) or throughout the year in south, 3–4 cubs born after gestation of 100 days; cubs dependent on mother for 18 months.

OTHER INFORMATION: live solitary lives in distinct territories, those of males overlapping several females. Lifespan 15 years (to 20 in captivity).

CONSERVATION STATUS: endangered.

CHEETAH

Acinonyx jubatus

Family: Felidae

THE CHEETAH IS THE FASTEST-MOVING LAND ANIMAL, *reaching speeds of up to 101 km (63 mi) per hour over short distances.*

DISTRIBUTION: now restricted to parts of Africa, Iran and adjacent areas of Turkmenistan, Afghanistan and Pakistan; originally more widespread.

SIZE: HB 1.12–1.5 m (44–59 in); TL 600–800 mm (23–31 in); SH 700–900 mm (27–35 in); WT 35–72 kg (77–159 lb). Males usually larger than females.

FORM: coat tawny with small round black spots; a black stripe runs from corner of eye down side of snout. More lightly built than other big cats.

DIET: small to medium-sized mammals, especially gazelles, small antelope and the young of larger antelope.

BREEDING: 1–5 cubs born after a gestation of 91–95 days. Cubs stay with mother for up to 22 months.

OTHER INFORMATION: females solitary, except when they have cubs; males may form small groups. Roam large areas in search of prey. Live about 15 years in the wild, up to 17 years in captivity.

CONSERVATION STATUS: threatened throughout its range, especially in Asia, by loss of habitat, which leads it to attack livestock, for which it is persecuted. Also killed for its skin. The Asiatic subspecies is endangered.

LEOPARD

Panthera pardus

Family: Felidae

THE LEOPARD OFTEN AMBUSHES *its prey, leaping down on it from the lower branches of a tree.*

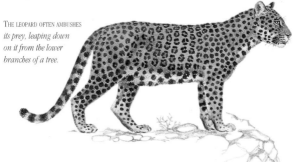

DISTRIBUTION: widespread throughout Africa, south of the Sahara and in southern Asia.

SIZE: HB 0.9–1.9 m (3–6.3 ft); TL 580–1,100 mm (22.6–42.9 in); SH 450–780 mm (17.5–30.4 in); WT males 37–90 kg (82–198 lb), females 28–60 kg (62–132 lb).

FORM: coat pale brown with black spots, small on head, large on belly, and in rosette patterns on back, flanks and upper limbs. Occasionally black panthers are found.

DIET: small to medium-sized hoofed mammals such as antelope, deer, sheep, goats; monkeys, hares, rodents; some ground-dwelling birds and occasionally fruit.

BREEDING: 1–6 cubs born after a gestation of 90–105 days. Live up to 15 years in the wild, over 25 in captivity.

OTHER INFORMATION: very strong—will drag large carcasses into trees, where it can feed undisturbed. When not hunting, the leopard often dozes stretched out on the branch of a tree.

CONSERVATION STATUS: widespread, but threatened by habitat loss, retaliation for its raids on livestock and hunting for its skin and for trophies. Many local subspecies are endangered.

SNOW LEOPARD

Panthera uncia

Ounce, Irbis
Family: Felidae

THE SNOW LEOPARD IS A SECRETIVE, SOLITARY ANIMAL *of the high mountains. Prey is scarce, so each leopard needs to hunt in a wide area.*

DISTRIBUTION: high mountains of Asia, including the Himalayas, Altai and Hindu Kush.

SIZE: HB 1.0–1.3 m (3.3–4.3 ft); TL 0.8–1.0 m (2.6–3.3 ft); SH 0.6 m (1.37 ft); WT 25–75 kg (55–165 lb).

FORM: coat long and thick, pale gray to smoky-gray, whitish on underparts; black or brown spots on head, neck and lower limbs; dark rings or rosettes, often enclosing smaller spots on back, flanks, upper limbs and tail. Build heavy, with long tail and large paws.

DIET: mammals such as ibex, wild sheep and goats, Musk ox, wild boar, hares and rodents; also large birds such as pheasants and ptarmigan.

BREEDING: 1–4 kittens after a gestation of 90–103 days, reared in a rocky shelter lined with fur.

OTHER INFORMATION: live up to 19 years in captivity.

CONSERVATION STATUS: endangered by poaching for its fur and by persecution for its attacks on domestic livestock as human settlement encroaches on its natural habitat.

BOBCAT

Felis rufus

Red lynx
Family: Felidae

THE BOBCAT CREEPS UP
*on its prey until it gets
close enough to pounce.
It covers as much as 3 m
(10 ft) in a single leap.*

DISTRIBUTION: North America, from southern Canada to central Mexico. Found in a wide range of habitats, from desert, mountains or rocky scree to swamps, thickets and forests.

SIZE: HB 0.65–1.0 m (2.1–3.3 ft); TL 110–190 mm (4.3–7.4 in); SH 450–580 mm (17.5–22.6 in); WT 4.1–15.3 kg (9–34 lb).

FORM: coat ranges from yellowish-buff to brown or reddish-brown, marked with dark spots and lines, denser on crown; underparts white; tail and backs of ears black-tipped; a ruff of fur extends down sides of cheeks.

DIET: mainly hares and cottontail rabbits, but also rodents, deer, livestock, bats, birds and other small vertebrates.

BREEDING: 1–6 kittens born in winter after a gestation of 60–70 days.

OTHER INFORMATION: the bobcat is a solitary nocturnal animal that hunts mainly on the ground, but also climbs trees to survey its territory or to escape its enemy, the wolf. Individual bobcats occupy territories that are marked out by scent deposited in urine and feces, and rubbed from glands on to trees and other objects. Each bobcat hunts an area of 1–110 sq km (0.4–38.6 sq mi)

CONSERVATION STATUS: not at risk.

PUMA

Felis concolor

Cougar, Mountain lion,
Panther
Family: Felidae

DISTRIBUTION: North and South
America, from south Yukon and
Nova Scotia to southern Chile and
Patagonia. Found in almost every kind
of habitat that offers cover.

SIZE: HB 0.97–1.96 m (3.2–6.4 ft);
TL 534–784 mm (21–31 in); SH 560–
780 mm (22–30 in); WT 36–103 kg
(79–227 lb). Males are larger than
females.

FORM: coat ranges from grayish-brown
to black; young cubs are spotted.

DIET: mainly Mule deer, young elk
and other hoofed mammals; also mice,
rats and squirrels.

BREEDING: 2–4 kittens born after a
gestation of 90–96 days.

*THE PUMA IS A POWERFUL PREDATOR. IT STALKS ITS
prey, then pounces or, if the prey is large,
leaps onto its back. It takes mainly old or sick
animals, so it helps to keep prey populations
healthy.*

OTHER INFORMATION: lives up to 18
years. Hunts over a wide area–up to
300 sq km (116 sq mi).

CONSERVATION STATUS: persecuted to
extinction by livestock farmers in the
eastern United States and Canada, but
not threatened in its remaining habitat.
The Florida and Eastern subspecies are
both endangered as a result of past
persecution.

12

GRAY WOLF

Canis lupus

Wolf, Timber wolf, White wolf
Family: Canidae

THE GRAY WOLF HUNTS IN A PACK AND OFTEN TRIES *to run down its prey over short distances. It reaches speeds of 70 km (43 mi) per hour and can pounce on prey from 5 m (16 ft) away.*

DISTRIBUTION: throughout much of the northern hemisphere, excluding desert and tropical forest habitats.

SIZE: HB 1.0–1.6 m (3.4–5.25 ft); TL 350–560 mm (14–22 in); SH 660–810 mm (25–32 in); WT 12–80 kg (27–176 lb); males usually larger than females.

FORM: coat grayish to tawny-buff with paler underparts; some individuals may be reddish-brown or black, coat tends to be paler in northern regions.

DIET: mammals such as deer, moose, caribou/reindeer, bison/buffalo, Musk ox, mountain sheep, rabbits, hares and beavers; also carrion and fruits.

BREEDING: 4–7 cubs born in later winter after a gestation of 61–63 days.

OTHER INFORMATION: live in packs of up to 20 animals. Dominance in the pack is established by threatening behavior and fighting.

CONSERVATION STATUS: numbers greatly reduced throughout its range. The Mexican subspecies is endangered.

Coyote

Canis latrans

Prairie wolf, Brush wolf
Family: Canidae

Distribution: North and Central America, from northern Alaska and western and central Canada south to Costa Rica. During the last 100 years the coyote has spread from its natural prairie habitat into southern Canada, perhaps helped by the reduction in wolf numbers due to persecution.

Size: HB 0.75–1.0 m (2.5–3.3 ft); TL 300–400 mm (12–16 in); SH 450–530 mm (18–21in); WT 10–18 kg (22–40 lb); males are usually larger than females.

Form: coat buff-gray with streaks of silver-gray; throat and belly white; muzzle, outer parts of ears, forelegs and feet dull brownish-yellow; black patches on forelegs and tip of tail.

COYOTES ARE CUNNING, OPPORTUNIST PREDATORS *that hunt in pairs or small family packs. A coyote will sometimes team up with an American badger: the coyote uses its acute sense of smell to find rodent burrows, and the badger excavates them.*

Diet: mostly small mammals such as rabbits, ground squirrels and mice, but groups of coyotes may hunt larger prey including livestock.

Breeding: 5–7 cubs born in spring after a gestation of about 63 days.

Other information: live for up to 15 years in captivity. The young may remain with their parents to help rear the next litter of cubs.

Conservation status: not at risk.

SILVERBACKED JACKAL

Canis mesomelas

Blackbacked jackal
Family: Canidae

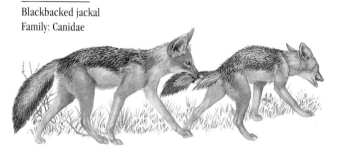

THE SILVERBACKED JACKAL IS A GREAT SCAVENGER, *taking advantage of the kills of other animals, such as lions, and of natural deaths on the savanna. It also hunts for itself, taking insects and small vertebrates, but a group can bring down a small antelope.*

DISTRIBUTION: Africa, in dry grassland and open woodland from Sudan to South Africa.

SIZE: HB 680–745 mm (26.5–29 in); TL 300–380 mm (12–15 in); SH 450–500 mm (18–20 in); WT 7–13.5 kg (15.5–30 lb); males slightly larger and heavier than females.

FORM: coat russet-brown, with white-rimmed black saddle streaked with silver-gray, extending down the tail, which is black-tipped.

DIET: mainly small mammals such as rodents, insects; carrion fruits and berries; occasionally kill larger prey such as small antelope.

BREEDING: 3–6 cubs born after a gestation of about 60 days. The young may remain with their parents for up to two years, helping to rear subsequent litters.

OTHER INFORMATION: lifespan up to 14 years in captivity. Silverbacked jackals live in pairs and small family groups; greater numbers may gather around large carcasses.

CONSERVATION STATUS: not at risk, but it is persecuted in sheep-rearing areas for attacks on livestock.

RED FOX

Vulpes vulpes

Silver fox, Cross fox
Family: Canidae

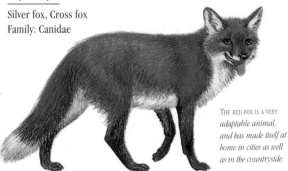

THE RED FOX IS A VERY *adaptable animal, and has made itself at home in cities as well as in the countryside.*

DISTRIBUTION: throughout most of the northern hemisphere, from the southern ranges of the Arctic circle to the deserts of central America and North Africa and the steppes of Asia.

SIZE: HB 455–900 mm (18–35 in); TL 300–555 mm (12–22 in); SH 350–450 mm (14–18 in); WT 3–14 kg (6.6–31 lb); males usually slightly larger and heavier than females.

FORM: coat varies from yellowish-red to rusty-red or brighter, with white, gray or black underparts; lower legs often black; tail tip often black or white. About 25% have a dark cross on their backs.

DIET: small mammals such as rabbits and rodents; birds, insects, earthworms, carrion, fruits and berries.

BREEDING: 4–7 cubs are born after a gestation of 51–53 days.

OTHER INFORMATION: usually solitary, but lives in pairs during the breeding season. Lifespan about 7 years in the wild, up to 15 years in captivity. It hunts mainly at night, especially near human settlements, relying on its acute senses to find its prey.

CONSERVATION STATUS: persecuted by farmers and hunted for sport, but not threatened as a species.

ARCTIC FOX

Alopex lagopus

Polar fox, Blue fox, White fox
Family: Canidae

THE ARCTIC FOX HUNTS ON THE *tundra in summer, but may move to the sea ice or farther inland in winter in search of food.*

DISTRIBUTION: circumpolar on the tundra and frozen ocean of Arctic latitudes.

SIZE: HB 458–675 mm (18–26 in); TL 255–425 mm (9.9–17 in); SH 280 mm (11 in); WT 1.4–9.0 kg (3–20 lb).

FORM: coat thick and wooly; there are two main color forms: a white coat that turns gray-brown in summer, and a pale bluish-gray coat that turns dark bluish-gray in winter.

DIET: small and medium-sized mammals, such as lemmings and baby seals; also sea birds and their eggs, fish, insects and other invertebrates, and berries. It also scavenges on carrion.

BREEDING: 2–25 young (usually 6–12) born in spring or early summer after a gestation of 49–57 days.

OTHER INFORMATION: lives for only a few years in the wild, but up to 15 years in captivity. The white-coated form is farmed for its fur, and forms an important part of the economy of native peoples in the Arctic.

CONSERVATION STATUS: not at risk.

17

POLAR BEAR

Ursus maritimus

Family: Ursidae

DISTRIBUTION: circumpolar in Arctic regions around the North Pole.

SIZE: HB 2.0–3.0 m (6.5–9.8 ft); TL 70–127 mm (3–5 in); SH up to 1.6 m (5.25 ft); WT 150–800 kg (330–176 lb); males larger than females.

FORM: coat white, sometimes stained yellow by seal oil.

DIET: mainly seals, walruses, carrion (especially stranded whales) and human garbage; also eats grasses, herbs and berries.

BREEDING: 1–3 cubs born in winter after a gestation of about 8 months. Female digs a snow den in which to give birth during hibernation.

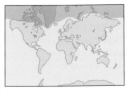

THE POLAR BEAR LIVES AND HUNTS MAINLY ON THE *sea ice, but ventures inland to breed. It is a very powerful swimmer.*

OTHER INFORMATION: only females hibernate. Cubs stay with their mother for at least 2 years.

CONSERVATION STATUS: threatened by persecution for its approaches to human settlements (attracted by garbage), and by pollution from oil industry. Legally protected throughout most of its range.

BROWN BEAR

Ursus arctos

Grizzly bear
Family: Ursidae

THE BROWN BEAR'S RANGE *once extended to Mexico, North Africa and Japan, but it has been much reduced by persecution.*

DISTRIBUTION: northwest North America, northern Europe and the mountains of southern Europe, the Middle East and central Asia.

SIZE: HB 1.7–3.0 m (5.6–10 ft); TL 60–210 mm (2–8 in); SH 0.9–1.5 m (3–5 ft); WT 150–780 kg (330–1720 lb); males larger than females.

FORM: coat ranges from cream to black, usually brown, often with white-tipped hairs ("grizzled").

DIET: a true omnivore: eats grasses, herbs, fruits, berries, nuts and seeds; insects and honey; rodents; fish; carrion; occasionally young hoofed mammals and livestock.

BREEDING: 1–4 cubs born in late winter after a gestation of 210–255 days.

OTHER INFORMATION: lives up to 30 years in the wild, almost 50 in captivity. Brown bears hibernate during winter in some areas.

CONSERVATION STATUS: numbers severely reduced in most areas, especially in Europe, by hunting, persecution and loss of habitat.

AMERICAN BLACK BEAR

Ursus americanus

Kermodes bear, Glacier bear
Family: Ursidae

THROUGHOUT THE WINTER *the American black bear hibernates for short periods, usually in a hollow log, under a fallen tree or in an abandoned burrow.*

DISTRIBUTION: North America, from Alaska and the Great Lakes to northern California and Mexico, mainly in forested areas.

SIZE: HB 1.3–1.8 m (4.25–6 ft); TL 120 mm (4–5 in); SH 800–950 mm (31–37 in); WT 92–270 kg (203–595 lb); males larger than females.

FORM: coat ranges from chocolate-brown to cinnamon-brown or black, sometimes with a white chest patch.

DIET: a true omnivore: 70 % of its diet is plant material such as bulbs, tubers, young shoots, berries and nuts; honey; small mammals; fish; insects; carrion; occasionally young hoofed mammals or livestock; garbage.

BREEDING: 1–5 cubs born in winter after a gestation of 210–215 days. They remain with their mother for over a year.

OTHER INFORMATION: a forest dweller, and a good tree climber. Lives for about 30 years.

CONSERVATION STATUS: not threatened, but numbers have been greatly reduced by hunting for sport and by persecution, especially where it comes into conflict with humans.

SUN BEAR

Helarctos malayanus

Malayan sun bear
Family: Ursidae

THE SUN BEAR USES ITS LARGE CLAWS TO GET AT ITS *favorite foods by tearing open the nests of termites and wild bees.*

DISTRIBUTION: dense forests in southeast Asia.

SIZE: HB 1.0–1.4 m (3.3–4.6 ft); TL 30–70 mm (1–3in); SH 700 mm (27in); WT 27–65 kg (50–143 lb).

FORM: coat dark brown to black, often with a whitish or orange chest mark and pale grayish or orange fur on the muzzle. This is the smallest of the bear family, with a stocky body, large paws and large curved claws.

DIET: honey, insects and their larvae (especially termites), ground-dwelling birds, rodents, and plant material such as palm shoots and fruit.

BREEDING: 1–3 cubs born after a gestation of about 210 days.

OTHER INFORMATION: live almost 25 years in captivity. Active mainly at night, spending the day sleeping or sunbathing in a tree.

CONSERVATION STATUS: threatened by destruction of its forest habitat.

COATI

Nasua nasua

Family: Procyonidae

COATIS FORAGE ON THE GROUND, *sniffing out underground insects and eggs, then using their paws to dig them out. They nest in trees, using their long tails for balancing as they climb.*

DISTRIBUTION: wooded areas of North and South America from Arizona to Panama, and east of the Andes to northern Argentina and Uruguay.

SIZE: HB 410–670 mm (16–26 in); TL 320–690 mm (12.5–27 in); SH up to 305 mm (12 in); WT 3–6 kg (6.5–13 lb).

FORM: coat tawny-red with black face; small white spot above and below each eye, and large one on each cheek; white throat and underparts; black feet and black rings on tail.

DIET: invertebrates such as ants, termites, beetles, grubs, spiders, scorpions, centipedes and land crabs; sometimes frogs, lizards and mice; eggs of turtles and lizards; also fruits.

BREEDING: 2–7 young born in a tree nest after a gestation of 70–77 days.

OTHER INFORMATION: lifespan about 14 years. It hunts mainly in the daytime. Females and young males live in groups of up to 20 animals; older males are solitary.

CONSERVATION STATUS: not at risk.

RACCOON

Procyon lotor

Coon
Family: Procyonidae

DISTRIBUTION: forest and scrub areas from North and Central America, from southern Canada to Panama.

SIZE: HB 415–600 mm (16–23 in); TL 200–405 mm (8–16 in); SH 228–304 mm (9–12 in); WT 2–12 kg (4.5–26 lb); males are usually larger than females.

FORM: coat color varies from grizzled to pale gray or reddish-gray; tail has alternate brown and black rings; black face mask with gray or whitish bars above and below; black patches around eyes; ears light-tipped.

DIET: a true omnivore: eats small animals such as rodents, frogs and lizards; young birds, eggs; fish, crayfish and crabs; fruits, berries and nuts.

THE RACCOON IS A VERY ADAPTABLE ANIMAL AND HAS *invaded human settlements, where it emerges at dusk to forage in garbage cans. It uses its sensitive hands to sort its food and may even wash it before feeding.*

BREEDING: 1–7 young born in a den in a hollow tree after a gestation of 60–73 days.

OTHER INFORMATION: raccoons do not hibernate, but in northern regions they may spend much of the winter in their dens, which are usually in hollow trees or abandoned burrows. A female and her offspring often hunt independently but den together.

CONSERVATION STATUS: not at risk.

23

GIANT PANDA

Ailuropoda melanoleuca

Family: Ursidae or Ailuropodidae

DISTRIBUTION: once found in much of eastern China, but now confined to the Sichuan, Shaaxi and Gansu provinces.

SIZE: HB 1.2–1.5 m (3.9–4.9 ft);
TL 100–150 mm (3.9–5.9 in);
SH 500–800 mm (19.5–41.2 in);
WT 75–160 kg (165–353 lb).

FORM: coat white, with black ears, eye patches, muzzle, limbs and shoulders.

DIET: mainly bamboo shoots and some herbs, bulbs and corms; also fish, small rodents and pikas.

BREEDING: 1–3 young born in September after a gestation of 125–150 days; usually only one survives.

THE GIANT PANDA IS A VEGETARIAN DESCENDED FROM *a line of meat-eaters. It can digest only about 20 per cent of its food and produces up to 9 kg (20 lb) of droppings a day, so it has to spend most of its waking hours eating.*

OTHER INFORMATION: lives up to 30 years in captivity.

CONSERVATION STATUS: highly endangered, mainly because of loss of habitat and hunting for its fur; the situation is exacerbated by its slow breeding rate and a reluctance to leave its home area.

COMMON WEASEL

Mustela nivalis

Least weasel,
European common weasel
Family: Mustelidae

THE WEASEL IS A FIERCE PREDATOR
*that often tracks prey to its
burrow and attacks it there.
The weasel's thin body can pass through
the narrow burrows of mice and voles.
If threatened, it will attack rather than flee.*

DISTRIBUTION: throughout the northern hemisphere from the Arctic to the edge of the subtropics.

SIZE: HB 110–260 mm (4.25–10 in); TL 17–80 mm (0.6–3 in); WT 25–250 g (0.87–8.7 oz); males larger than females. Eurasian animals are usually larger than North American ones.

FORM: coat reddish-brown with white underparts separated by a clear demarcation line; may have dark blotches on underparts; tail reddish-brown. In north of range, coat turns white in winter.

DIET: small vertebrates such as mice, voles, birds, lizards and frogs.

BREEDING: 4–10 young born at any time of year after a gestation of 34–37 days. Many produce more than one litter in a year.

OTHER INFORMATION: lives for about one year. An athletic animal, good at running, climbing and swimming. The weasel is smaller than its relative the stoat and has no black tip to its tail.

CONSERVATION STATUS: not at risk.

25

EUROPEAN POLECAT

Mustela putorius

Polecat, Common polecat,
Forest polecat
Family: Mustelidae

THE POLECAT IS A SECRETIVE NOCTURNAL
*hunter that sleeps in its den by
day. If attacked, it screams and
gives off a foul smell.*

DISTRIBUTION: throughout Europe,
north to southern Sweden and southern
Finland, and east across Russia to the
Ural Mountains.

SIZE: HB 295–460 mm (11.5–18 in);
TL 80–190 mm (3–7.4 in); WT 0.2–
1.4 kg (0.4–3 lb).

FORM: coat buff to black with a dark
mask across the eyes; underparts pale
yellow; often whitish around mouth
and chin, and between eyes and ears.

DIET: small vertebrates, mainly mice,
rats and rabbits; also birds, snakes,
frogs, fish and eggs; occasionally raids
chicken coops.

BREEDING: 4–12 young born in spring
or early summer after a gestation of
40–42 days. They leave their mother
after 3 months.

OTHER INFORMATION: lifespan of up
to 6 years in the wild. The European
polecat was the ancestor of the domesticated ferret used for hunting rabbits.

CONSERVATION STATUS: not at risk; at
present numbers are increasing, follow-
ing a reduction in persecution by
gamekeepers.

FISHER

Martes pennanti

Pekan, Virginian polecat
Family: Mustelidae

DISTRIBUTION: mountainous forest areas of North America, from southern Yukon and Labrador to California, Utah, the Great Lakes and Virginia.

SIZE: HB 470–750 mm (18–29 in); TL 300–420 mm (12–16 in); WT 1.3–5.5 kg (3–12 lb); males larger than females.

FORM: coat brown, with gold to silver hoariness on head and shoulders; legs and tail black; variable cream chest.

DIET: small mammals such as Snowshoe hares, squirrels, mice and tree porcupines; also birds, fish, insects, eggs; carrion; fruits, berries and nuts.

THE FISHER HUNTS SMALL MAMMALS, BOTH ON THE *ground and in the trees. It can even kill tree porcupines by attacking their unprotected faces until they go into shock, and can be turned over exposing their unquilled bellies.*

BREEDING: 1–6 young born in spring after a gestation of 10–12 months.

OTHER INFORMATION: lifespan of up to 10 years. A good climber of trees. Despite its name, fish form only a very small part of its diet.

CONSERVATION STATUS: not at risk, but numbers have been greatly reduced by past trapping for the fur trade.

HOODED SKUNK

Mephitis macroura

Long-tailed skunk
Family: Mustelidae

DISTRIBUTION: woodland, grassland and desert from Arizona and southwest Texas to Costa Rica.

SIZE: HB 280–380 mm (11–15 in); TL 185–435 mm (7–17 in); WT 0.7–2.5 kg (1.5–5.5 lb).

FORM: coat black with white head, back and tail; the white areas have black hairs mixed with them; there may be a faint white stripe on each flank and a white stripe on the snout. Some animals have a black head.

DIET: small rodents; birds, eggs; insects, worms; fruits and berries.

BREEDING: mates in February. 1–10 young born in the early summer after a gestation of 59–77 days. They leave their mother in the fall.

THE SKUNK IS FAMOUS FOR ITS THREATENING *displays. It arches its back, raises its tail and aims a foul spray of acrid liquid at the attacker from glands under the tail. The smell can be detected 2.5 km (1.5 mi) away.*

OTHER INFORMATION: lifespan about 6 years in the wild, over 12 in captivity. Active mainly at night, resting by day in the shelter of a bush or burrow. Females with young change burrows frequently. Skunks are valuable predators of mice, rats and insects, but may sometimes attack poultry, and are reported to carry rabies.

CONSERVATION STATUS: not at risk.

28

EUROPEAN RIVER OTTER

Lutra lutra

European otter, Eurasian otter, Common otter
Family: Mustelidae

THE EUROPEAN RIVER OTTER IS HIGHLY ADAPTED FOR *its aquatic lifestyle, with a sleek, streamlined body, small ears and webbed feet. The ears and nostrils can be closed while submerged. Its sensitive whiskers can detect slight water movements caused by nearby fish.*

DISTRIBUTION: Europe and Asia, from western Europe south to northwest Africa, and east to Siberia, Korea, Indochina and southeast Asia.

SIZE: HB 550–950 mm (21–37 in); TL 300–550 mm (12–22 in); WT 5–12 kg (11–26 lb).

FORM: coat chestnut-brown to dark brown, with creamy underparts.

DIET: mainly fish, frogs, crayfish, crabs and other aquatic invertebrates; also takes birds and small mammals such as rabbits and rodents.

BREEDING: 2–5 young born after a gestation of 61–63 days. Breeding is seasonal in the north of its range, non-seasonal elsewhere. The female raises the young alone in a den ("holt") in the riverbank or under tree roots.

OTHER INFORMATION: lifespan in captivity is up to 22 years. They mark their territories with scent.

CONSERVATION STATUS: not at risk, but numbers have been drastically reduced in many parts of its range as a result of habitat destruction, disturbance by humans and pollution.

SPOT-NECKED OTTER

Lutra maculicollis

Family: Mustelidae

A SPOT-NECKED OTTER'S FEET ARE *webbed almost to the tips of its toes. Its powerful tail is used as a rudder when swimming. It can stay underwater for up to 8 minutes.*

DISTRIBUTION: Africa south of the Sahara, except in desert areas.

SIZE: HB 660–790 mm (26–31 in); TL 330–450 mm (13–16 in); WT up to 14 kg (31 lb); males usually larger than females.

FORM: coat very dark umber, with slightly paler underparts; throat and/or groin usually with irregular patches and spots of creamy-white.

DIET: mainly fish, frogs, crayfish, crabs and other aquatic invertebrates; also small vertebrates such as frogs, birds and rodents.

BREEDING: 1–4 young after a gestation of about 61–63 days. Young remain with mother for about a year.

OTHER INFORMATION: may be seen by day, but is usually most active at night. This species is often trapped in fishing nets. It is sometimes considered to belong to a separate genus, *Hydrictis*.

CONSERVATION STATUS: although its distribution is fragmented, the Spot-necked otter is not threatened, except in South Africa, where the local population is endangered.

30

EURASIAN BADGER

Meles meles

European badger
Family: Mustelidae

BADGERS FORAGE MAINLY AFTER DARK, RELYING ON _smell to find food. They love to play games, including leap frog!_

DISTRIBUTION: wooded and forested areas of Europe and Asia, from the British Isles and southern Scandinavia south to China and Japan.

SIZE: HB 670–810 mm (26–32 in); TL 150–200 mm (6–8 in); WT 10–12 kg (22–26 lb).

FORM: coat grizzle grayish-black, with black underparts, legs and feet; head and ear tips white; black facial stripe from snout through eyes to behind ears; tail white or pale in male, grayer in female.

DIET: small vertebrates such as birds, rodents, lizards, frogs; also eggs; invertebrates including insects, earthworms and snails; fruits, berries, roots, cereals and nuts.

BREEDING: 2–6 young born after a gestation of up to a year.

OTHER INFORMATION: lifespan up to 16 years in captivity. Live in large communal burrow systems called setts. In the colder parts of their range, they may sleep for several months in winter, but do not hibernate properly.

CONSERVATION STATUS: not at risk.

31

COMMON PALM CIVET

Paradoxurus hermaphroditus

Toddy cat
Family: Viverridae

THE COMMON PALM CIVET IS A TREE DWELLER. *Its nickname of "toddy cat" comes from its fondness for the fermented palm juice ("toddy") collected by local people in bamboo tubes attached to palm trunks.*

back and small to medium spots on sides and base of tail; face mask of spots and forehead streak; tail tip sometimes white.

DISTRIBUTION: forested areas of southeast Asia, from Kashmir to Sri Lanka, southeastern China, the Malay Peninsula, Sumatra, Java, Borneo, Sulawesi, the Philippines, and many other small islands.

SIZE: HB 432–710 mm (17–28 in); TL 406–660 mm (16–26 in); WT 1.5–4.5 kg (3.3–10 lb).

FORM: coat color varies from buff to dark brown; usually black stripes on

DIET: small invertebrates including insects; fruit and seeds.

BREEDING: 2–5 young per litter. Gestation period unknown.

OTHER INFORMATION: lifespan up to 22 years in captivity. Usually nocturnal. Introduced to some areas to control rats.

CONSERVATION STATUS: not at risk.

COMMON GENET

Genetta genetta

Small-spotted genet,
European genet
Family: Viverridae

THE COMMON GENET IS A SILENT,
*stealthy nocturnal predator
that stalks its prey both on the
ground and in the trees. Its flexible body
can squeeze into narrow crevices in search
of mice, rats and other small animals.*

DISTRIBUTION: grasslands and forests
of southern Europe (in France and the
Iberian Peninsula), the Middle East,
and Africa south of the Sahara.

SIZE: HB 400–630 mm (16–25 in);
TL 370–520 mm (14–20 in); WT 1.0–
2.3 kg (2.2–5.0 lb).

FORM: coat grayish-white with rows
of blackish spots; tail has 9–10 dark
rings and a white tip; prominent dark
spinal crest.

DIET: small vertebrates such as mice,
birds and lizards; insects, spiders and
other invertebrates; eggs and fruits.
Occasionally game birds and poultry.

BREEDING: 1–3 young born
after a gestation of 70–77 days,
sometimes less; may produce two
litters a year.

OTHER INFORMATION: lifespan over
22 years in captivity. Usually live alone
or in pairs. Mainly nocturnal, spending
the day in a rock crevice, hollow tree,
old burrow or on a large branch.

CONSERVATION STATUS: not at risk.

33

NARROW-STRIPED MONGOOSE

Mungotictis decemlineata

Malagasy narrow-striped mongoose
Family: Viverridae

DISTRIBUTION: sandy, open savannas of western and southwestern Madagascar.

SIZE: HB 250–350 mm (10–14 in); TL 230–270 mm (9–10.5 in); WT 600–700 g (1.3–1.5 lb).

FORM: coat brownish-gray with speckling on back and sides; 10 to 12 narrow reddish-brown to dark brown longitudinal stripes on back and sides. Underparts pale beige.

DIET: insects and other invertebrates; small vertebrates and bird eggs. Eggs and snails are thrown at the ground until they break.

THE NARROW-STRIPED MONGOOSE OF MADAGASCAR *is at home on dry land and in water. Its feet are partly webbed and it is a good swimmer, but it also spends much of its time in trees.*

BREEDING: a single young born after gestation of 90–105 days. Young stays with its mother for about 2 years.

OTHER INFORMATION: active by day, spending the night in tree holes during the wet summer and in ground burrows in the dry winter. In summer lives in large groups, but in winter lives alone, in pairs or in smaller groups.

CONSERVATION STATUS: not persecuted, but at risk by rapid habitat destruction. Other species occur throughout Africa and Asia, and are not endangered.

SPOTTED HYENA

Crocuta crocuta

Laughing hyena
Family: Hyaenidae

THE SPOTTED HYENA'S POWERFUL JAWS ENABLE IT TO *crush and eat the bones and skin of its prey. During communal hunts it can reach speeds of 50 km (30 mi) per hour.*

DISTRIBUTION: grassland and open country in Africa south of the Sahara, except in the Congo basin.

SIZE: HB 0.95–1.66 m (3–5.4 ft); TL 255–360 mm (10–14 in); SH 700–915 mm (27–36 in); WT 40–86 kg (88–190 lb); females usually longer and heavier than males.

FORM: coat short, yellow to red, irregular dark brown oval spots; mane short; tail with brush of long black hairs.

DIET: any medium-sized hoofed mammals, but especially wildebeest (takes mainly very young or very old animals) and carrion.

BREEDING: 1–3 young born after a gestation of about 110 days.

OTHER INFORMATION: they live in groups ("clans") of up to 80 animals, subdivided into smaller groups.

CONSERVATION STATUS: numbers have declined and it is already extinct in parts of Africa; persecuted for its attacks on livestock and game.

35

AMAZON DOLPHIN

Inia geoffrensis

Bouto
Family: Iniidae

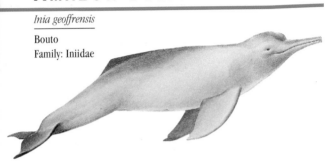

THIS FRESHWATER DOLPHIN USES ECHOLOCATION AND *a highly sensitive snout to hunt for fish. It emits high-frequency sounds, then analyzes the echoes to locate objects in the water.*

DIET: fish up to about 300 mm (1 ft) long; also shrimps.

BREEDING: only one young born at a time, after a gestation of about 1 year.

DISTRIBUTION: in the fresh water of the Amazon and Orinoco river systems of Brazil, Venezuela and Colombia, and the Madeira river system of Bolivia, as far as 2,800 km (1,740 mi) up-river from the sea. May migrate into flooded forest areas at high water.

SIZE: HB 1.7–3.0 m (5.6–10 ft); WT 71–120 kg (157–265 lb).

FORM: color dark bluish-gray above, pink (sometimes bright pink) on belly and sides, darker in Orinoco subspecies. Younger animals more silvery below. Head rounded with slender beak; eyes small. Blowhole transverse, crescent-shaped. Dorsal fin forms a long ridge.

OTHER INFORMATION: the Amazon dolphin lives in small groups within a specific territory. It uses echolocation to detect obstacles and prey in muddy waters and probes the river bed with its snout to disturb fish. Sensory bristles along the beak enhance its sense of touch. It makes a variety of sounds of unknown significance.

CONSERVATION STATUS: endangered as a result of hunting, water pollution, disruption of habitat due to hydroelectric dams and injury from motor boats.

KILLER WHALE

Orcinus orca

Orca
Family: Delphinidae

DISTRIBUTION: in all seas and oceans worldwide, from the poles to the tropics.

SIZE: HB 6.5–8.0 m (21–26 ft); WT 2.5–9.0 tonnes (2.5–8.85 tons); males are larger than females.

FORM: color black on back and flanks; belly white extending as a lobe up the flanks; white oval patch above and behind eye; indistinct gray saddle over back behind dorsal fin. Dorsal fin erect, triangular, up to 1.8 m (5.9 ft) high, smaller and backwardly curved in female. Pectoral and tail flukes broad.

DIET: fish, squid, seals, dolphins, porpoises and whales; also sea turtles and penguins. Hunt cooperatively and will herd shoals of fish together.

BY HUNTING IN A PACK, *Killer whales can tackle large prey such as seals, dolphins and even large whales, but they eat mainly fish and squid. They will turn over ice floes and even beach themselves to attack resting seals.*

BREEDING: only one young born at a time, throughout year, after a gestation of 16–17 months.

OTHER INFORMATION: lifespan at least 50 years. Lives in "pods" of 2–40 animals, led by a large male; these pods occasionally coalesce into larger schools of up to 250 animals.

CONSERVATION STATUS: not at risk.

BOTTLE-NOSED DOLPHIN

Tursiops truncatus

Family: Delphinidae

THE BOTTLE-NOSED DOLPHIN USES *a wide range of sounds to communicate and is thought to have a complex language.*

DISTRIBUTION: coastal waters and estuaries of the Atlantic Ocean and adjoining seas. The three species of bottle-nosed dolphin are sometimes counted as a single species; the other species are found in the Pacific and Indian Oceans and adjoining seas. Sometimes swims up large rivers.

SIZE: HB 2.3–3.1 m (7.5–10 ft); WT 150–275 kg (331–606 lb)). The distinctive "beak" is about 80 mm (3.2 in) long, and is said to resemble the top of an old-fashioned gin bottle – hence the dolphin's name.

FORM: color variable, usually dark gray on back, paler gray on flanks, fading to white or pink on belly; older animals may have spots on belly.

DIET: mainly bottom-dwelling fish.

BREEDING: only one young born at a time, after a gestation of about a year.

OTHER INFORMATION: lifespan over 35 years. Uses echolocation to navigate and find its food, emitting high frequency sounds and analyzing the echoes. It is highly intelligent, has a brain larger than the human brain, and can be trained to perform acrobatics, leaping out of the water to a height of up to 6 m (20 ft).

CONSERVATION STATUS: not at risk.

COMMON DOLPHIN

Delphinus delphis

Saddleback dolphin
Family: Delphinidae

THE COMMON DOLPHIN USES ITS LONG ROWS OF *pointed teeth to seize slippery fish and squid, which it then swallows whole. It is a fast swimmer, reaching speeds of up to 40 km (25 mi) per hour. Its slender torpedo-shaped body is suited to this life.*

DISTRIBUTION: worldwide in tropical, subtropical and warm temperate oceans and seas. Usually found well out to sea.

SIZE: HB 1.5–2.6 m (4.9–8.5 ft); WT 60–120 kg (132–265 lb).

FORM: coloration variable, usually brownish-black on back and upper flanks; underparts creamy-white to white; flanks have an hourglass pattern of tan or yellowish-tan, becoming paler and gray behind dorsal fin, where it may extend to dorsal surface; black stripe from flipper to middle of lower jaw and from eye to base of beak; flippers black to light gray or white. In some animals there may be one or two gray lines running longitudinally along the lower flanks.

DIET: fish, squid and prawns.

BREEDING: only one young born at a time every 2 or 3 years, after a gestation of 10–11 months. It is weaned at about 19 months.

OTHER INFORMATION: lifespan about 20 years. Lives in large schools of up to 100,000 animals.

CONSERVATION STATUS: not at risk, but numbers are declining because of over-hunting and drowning in fishing nets. Difficult to breed in captivity.

39

HARBOR PORPOISE

Phocoena phocoena

Common porpoise
Family: Phocoenidae

THE HARBOR PORPOISE
*travels in small schools
close to the water surface, rising
occasionally to let out stale air and
breath in fresh air through its blowhole,
which is shut tight when under water.*

DISTRIBUTION: coastal waters, large river mouths and estuaries of the north Atlantic from the Davis Strait, Iceland and Novaya Zemlya to North Carolina, the Cape Verde Islands and Gambia; the Mediterranean and Black Seas; and the north Pacific from Alaska to Japan and Baja California.

SIZE: HB 1.5–1.9 m (4.9–6.2 ft); WT 45–90 kg (99–198 lb).

FORM: color dark gray to black fading to whitish underparts, or black all over. The head is conical with no "beak".

DIET: mainly small to medium-sized fish such as herring, mackerel, sardines and cod, and probably squid, too. Individuals within groups split up while feeding.

BREEDING: only one young born at a time, after a gestation of about 10–11 months.

OTHER INFORMATION: lifespan up to 10 years, rarely 13. Thought to navigate and find its prey by echolocation.

CONSERVATION STATUS: once abundant, it is now probably endangered, as a result of becoming entangled in fishing nets, which it cannot detect by echolocation; other contributing factors include inshore pollution and a decline in its food supply as a result of humans overfishing.

BELUGA

Delphinapterus leucas

Belukha, White whale
Family: Monodontidae
or Delphinidae

THE BELUGA HAS BEEN NICKNAMED "THE SEA CANARY" *because it produces a wide range of sounds, including clicks, squeaks, yelps, whistles and liquid trills, which are so loud that they can be heard out of the water.*

DISTRIBUTION: coastal waters of the northern oceans around North America, Greenland, Europe (Scandinavia) and Russia. Some populations migrate regularly between distinct feeding grounds and breeding grounds, and to avoid build-ups of sea ice in winter.

SIZE: HB 4.0–6.5 m (13–21 ft); WT 0.5–1.4 tonnes (0.5–1.4 tons); males larger than females.

FORM: color white; young belugas are slate-gray to reddish-brown, but change to medium gray when 2 years old, and later to white. It has a very pronounced forehead or "melon," a blunt snout with no "beak" and no dorsal fin.

DIET: schooling fish, such as herring and cod, squid, cuttlefish, octopus and crustaceans.

BREEDING: only one young born at a time, after a gestation of about a year.

OTHER INFORMATION: lifespan up to 30 years. It is a good diver and can travel underwater for perhaps 2–3 km (1.25–1.9 mi) without surfacing.

CONSERVATION STATUS: not at risk, but overhunting has reduced numbers. The St. Lawrence river population is threatened by water pollution.

NARWHAL

Monodon monoceros

Family: Monodontidae

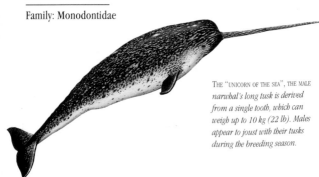

THE "UNICORN OF THE SEA", THE MALE *narwhal's long tusk is derived from a single tooth, which can weigh up to 10 kg (22 lb). Males appear to joust with their tusks during the breeding season.*

DISTRIBUTION: deep waters of Arctic oceans and seas, from North America and Greenland to Russia.

SIZE: HB 4.5–6.6 m (15–22 ft); WT 0.8–1.8 tonnes (0.8–1.8 tons).

FORM: color mottled grayish-green, cream and black, whitening with age from the belly up; young dark gray. The head is rounded, due to the pronounced forehead or "melon". There is no dorsal fin and the flippers curl upward and outward with age. The male has a single spirally-grooved tusk up to 2.7 m (8.6 ft) long arising from his snout. The other teeth are not properly developed.

DIET: bottom-dwelling fish such as flatfish, squid, shrimp, crabs and other crustaceans.

BREEDING: only one young born at a time after a gestation of about 14–15 months.

OTHER INFORMATION: lifespan up to 40 years. Lives in groups of 3–20 animals, but may gather in larger schools to migrate. An expert diver; several narwhals may cooperate to break through the sea ice (using their melons) to make breathing holes.

CONSERVATION STATUS: threatened by overhunting for its tusks and meat.

SPERM WHALE

Physeter catodon

Cachalot, Spermacet
Family: Physeteridae

THE SPERM WHALE IS THE WORLD'S DEEPEST-DIVING
mammal. It has been found at a depth of
1,134 m (3,720 ft), but is thought to reach
depths of over 3,000 m (9,840 ft). It can stay
underwater for almost 2 hours.

DISTRIBUTION: worldwide in polar and
temperate oceans and seas.

SIZE: HB 15–20 m (49–66 ft); WT 35
–50 tonnes (34–49 tonnes); males
often twice as large as females.

FORM: color dark gray with white
marks and circular scars, especially on
head. The head is huge and squarish.
There is no dorsal fin. The blowhole is
on the left side of the head near the tip
of the snout.

DIET: deep-sea squid, octopus, cuttlefish and fish.

BREEDING: only one calf born at a time
after a gestation of 14–16 months.

OTHER INFORMATION: lifespan over 70
years. The whale has up to 350 mm
(18 in) of blubber to insulate it against
the cold of the deep ocean. Its huge
head contains up to 1,900 liters (420
gallons) of oil. This oil may help trans-
mit high-frequency sounds for echolocation and communication, or it may
help in buoyancy control.

CONSERVATION STATUS: endangered,
mainly as a result of excessive hunting
for its spermaceti wax, oil (used as a
high-quality lubricant for machinery
and in ointments) and ambergris (a
substance found in the gut, which is
used in perfumes).

NORTHERN BOTTLENOSED WHALE

Hyperoodon ampullatus

Family: Ziphiidae

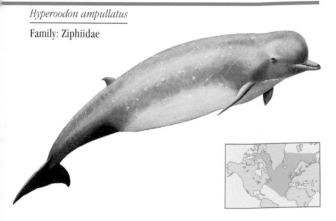

DISTRIBUTION: North Atlantic Ocean; migrates south to off Cape Verde and New York in winter. Usually stays in waters over 1,000 m (3,280 ft) deep, but may approach polar ice in summer.

SIZE: HB 7.5–10 m (25–33 ft); WT 3.5–5.0 tonnes (3.4–4.9 tons); males larger than females.

FORM: color variable, usually greenish-brown above, with smoke-gray belly, fading to cream all over with age; calves umber-brown to black. This species has a prominent, almost bulbous forehead, especially in the male, and a pronounced "beak".

DIET: mainly squid; also fish (mostly herring) and starfish.

THE NORTHERN BOTTLENOSED WHALE IS A DEEP SEA *diver, reaching depths of 1,000 m (3,280 ft) or more; it can stay under water for up to two hours. It uses a variety of clicks and whistles for echolocation of its prey and for communication.*

BREEDING: only one calf born at a time in spring, after a gestation of about a year; probably breeds only every 2 years.

OTHER INFORMATION: lifespan at least 37 years. Usually live in pairs or in small groups of similar-aged animals. As in the Sperm whale, the large forehead is filled with oil. A large male may yield up to 200 kg (440 lb) of spermaceti oil, and about 2,000 kg (4,400 lb) of blubber oil.

CONSERVATION STATUS: threatened.

GRAY WHALE

Eschrichtius robustus

Devil fish
Family: Eschrichtidae

THE GRAY WHALE FEEDS ON THE SEA BED BY *rolling on its side and pushing its head through the mud to stir up crustaceans and small fish. It sucks the water into its mouth, then forces it out.*

DISTRIBUTION: shallow coastal waters of Arctic and Pacific Oceans, from Chukchi, Beaufort and Bering Seas and Sea of Okhotsk south to Baja California and South Korea. Spends summer feeding in the Arctic, then migrates south to coastal bays and lagoons to breed.

SIZE: HB 12−15 m (39−49 ft); WT 25−34 tonnes (25−33 tons).

FORM: color mottled gray or black, usually covered in white patches of barnacles and whale lice. Dorsal fin absent, but has a series of low humps along the middle of the lower back. Throat has 2 or 3 short curving furrows.

DIET: bottom-dwelling crustaceans (mostly amphipods), mollusks and bristleworms, and small fish.

BREEDING: one calf born at a time in winter after 12−13 months' gestation.

OTHER INFORMATION: lifespan about 70 years. This is a baleen (whalebone) whale: it feeds by sieving the water through large plates of whalebone up to 450 mm (18 in) long hanging down from the upper jaw.

CONSERVATION STATUS: endangered; numbers reduced so drastically by past hunting that west Pacific population is now close to extinction.

45

HUMPBACK WHALE

Megaptera novaeangliae

Family: Balaenopteridae

*A HUMPBACK WHALE BREACHES —
it hurls itself out of the water,
then crashes back onto the surface with a loud splash that can
be heard a long way off. This
may be a form of display or
long-distance communication.*

DISTRIBUTION: worldwide in all oceans. Lives mainly out at sea, but migrates to shallow tropical waters for breeding.

SIZE: HB 12.5–17 m (41–56 ft); WT 30–45 tonnes (30–44 tons); females slightly larger than males.

FORM: color black above, with white grooves; undersides of flukes have variable white pattern; baleen (whalebone) plates dark gray.

DIET: mainly krill (shrimp-like crustaceans) and small fish; also squid and comb jellies (sea gooseberries).

BREEDING: only one calf born at a time, in winter, after a gestation of 11.5 months.

OTHER INFORMATION: lifespan about 80 years. This species is famous for its "songs", repeated sequences of sounds in complex patterns that can last for up to 35 minutes. The song is sung by single males during the breeding season, and varies from one population to another, like a dialect.

CONSERVATION STATUS: highly endangered as a result of overhunting; many whales also drown in fishing nets. In some areas they are in competition for food with commercial fishing boats.

MINKE WHALE

Balaenoptera acutorostrata

Piked whale
Family: Balaenopteridae

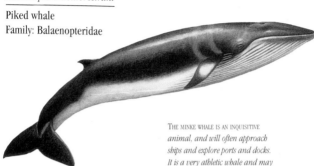

THE MINKE WHALE IS AN INQUISITIVE animal, and will often approach ships and explore ports and docks. It is a very athletic whale and may leap right out of the water.

DISTRIBUTION: most oceans and seas, especially the North Pacific, north Atlantic and Southern Ocean, seldom more than 150 km (93 mi) from land. Some populations make long migrations from polar feeding grounds to the tropics for the winter.

SIZE: HB 7.3–10 m (24–33ft); WT 6–10 tonnes (0.9–9.8 tons); females slightly larger than males.

FORM: color dark-gray above; belly and undersides of flippers white; pale streaks behind head; baleen (whalebone) plates yellowish-white, sometimes black. Flippers narrow and pointed; head bullet-shaped; dorsal fin high and backward-curving; series of 50–70 broad grooves run all the way from its chin to its belly.

DIET: small fish such as herring, sardines and cod; squid; plankton.

BREEDING: one calf born in winter or spring after a gestation of 10–10.5 months; breed only every 2 years.

OTHER INFORMATION: lifespan up to 50 years. Has a wide range of vocal sounds; individuals may have distinctive patterns of thumping sounds.

CONSERVATION STATUS: not at risk, but numbers reduced by overhunting.

BLUE WHALE

Balaenoptera musculus

Family: Balaenopteridae

Up to 35 m (115 ft) long and weighing up to 190 tonnes (187 tons), the Blue whale is the largest animal that has ever lived.

DISTRIBUTION: north Pacific, north Atlantic and Southern Oceans.

SIZE: HB averages 25–35 m (82–115 ft); WT usually 80–130 tonnes (79–113 tons), some heavier.

FORM: color mottled bluish-gray; flippers have pale undersides, often tinged yellow by microorganisms; baleen (whalebone) plates blue-black.

DIET: krill (shrimp-like crustaceans).

BREEDING: one calf (rarely twins) born in spring/summer, after 11–12 months' gestation; breed every 2 or 3 years. At birth, the calf is about 7 m (23 ft) long and weighs about 2 tonnes (2 tons).

OTHER INFORMATION: lifespan at least 70 years, and sometimes as much as

110. Lives alone or in small groups. At its summer feeding grounds it may consume up to 3.6 tonnes (3.5 tons) of krill a day. For the rest of the year it appears to live off stored fat. It makes the loudest natural sounds ever recorded; up to 188 decibels, they can be heard up to 850 km (528 mi) away.

CONSERVATION STATUS: highly endangered as a result of overhunting. It is thought that there may be only about 500 Blue whales left. A further threat is developing from large-scale harvesting of krill in the Southern Ocean.

RIGHT WHALE

Eubalaena glacialis

Family: Balaenidae

THIS WAS THE "RIGHT" WHALE TO HUNT: ITS LONG, *fine whalebone was used to make corsets, crinoline and taffeta, while the oil from its blubber was used for lamps, cooking, in lubricants and in soap.*

DISTRIBUTION: temperate waters of the Pacific, Atlantic and Indian Oceans and adjoining seas. Females migrate to shallow coastal bays to give birth.

SIZE: HB 13.6–18 m (45–59 ft); WT 50–95 tonnes (49–93 tons); males larger than females.

FORM: color black, with white patches on chin and belly; head and jaws have several large irregular skin callosities infested with whitish parasites, including one at the front of the upper jaw, often called the "bonnet"; baleen (whalebone) plates gray or grayish-yellow. Dorsal fin absent.

DIET: mainly krill; also other small crustaceans and small fish.

BREEDING: only one calf born at a time, in winter, after a gestation of about one year; breed only every 2 or 3 years.

OTHER INFORMATION: lifespan probably over 30 years. Individuals can be recognized by the pattern of their callosities.

CONSERVATION STATUS: highly endangered by hunting; almost extinct in the Atlantic. Other risks include fishing nets, water pollution and injury from boats.

BOWHEAD WHALE

Balaena mysticetus

Greenland right whale
Family: Balaenidae

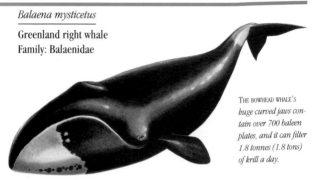

THE BOWHEAD WHALE'S *huge curved jaws contain over 700 baleen plates, and it can filter 1.8 tonnes (1.8 tons) of krill a day.*

DISTRIBUTION: Arctic Ocean off northwest Canada and Greenland, Hudson Bay, Gulf of St Lawrence, Bering Sea, Barents Sea and Sea of Okhotsk. Migrates to south of its range in winter.

SIZE: HB 15–20 m (48–64 ft); WT 60–100 tonnes (59–98 tons); males slightly larger than females.

FORM: color black; front of lower jaw creamy; belly may have white patches; base of tail sometimes gray. Dorsal fin absent; baleen plates gray to black; jaws highly curved.

DIET: krill (shrimp-like crustaceans) and other small crustaceans.

BREEDING: one calf born in spring or summer, after a gestation of about 13 months. Breeds only every 3–6 years.

OTHER INFORMATION: lifespan over 30 years. Lives alone or in small groups; larger groups may form on migration. Feeds mainly in summer, living off fat in winter. Produces a wide range of sounds, include hooting, humming, moans, purrs, roars and pulsed sounds. When surfacing, emits V-shaped spout of water vapor up to 7 m (20 ft) high.

CONSERVATION STATUS: highly endangered as a result of overhunting in the last century. Protected in most of its range, except for a small quota allotted to native peoples.

STELLER SEA LION

Eumetopias jubatus

Northern sea lion
Family: Otariidae

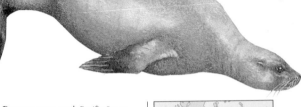

THE STELLER SEA LION, THE LARGEST *of the sea lions. The external ears distinguish sea lions and fur seals from "true" seals, but their small size helps to maintain streamlining.*

DISTRIBUTION: north Pacific Ocean from 66°N to the Sea of Japan and California.

SIZE: HB 2.4–2.9 m (8–9.5 ft); WT 273–1,000 kg (602–984 lb). Bulls much larger than females.

FORM: color ranges from light-brown to reddish-brown. Unlike seals, sea lions and fur seals can bend their hind flippers under the body, which makes them more mobile on land.

DIET: fish, especially flounders, halibut, rockfish and lamprey; also squid, octopus, clams and crabs. Will also take young seals and Sea otters.

BREEDING: only one young born at a time, in spring or early summer, after a gestation of 12 months. It is usually weaned at 8–11 months, but may continue to suckle for up to 3 years, until the next young is born. Bulls hold a harem of 10–20 females.

OTHER INFORMATION: lifespan about 23 years. These sea lions live in social groups and colonies gather to breed on the beaches of offshore islands.

CONSERVATION STATUS: not yet endangered, but numbers are decreasing as a result of disease, drowning in fishing nets and competition for food with commercial fisheries.

NORTHERN FUR SEAL

Callorhinus ursinus

Alaskan fur seal
Family: Otariidae

THE NORTHERN FUR SEAL HAS THE most valuable pelt of any seal. Its thick underfur contains some 57,000 hairs per sq cm (8,825,000 per sq in). It was hunted to the brink of extinction in the last century.

DISTRIBUTION: north Pacific Ocean, from the Sea of Okhotsk and the Bering Sea to the Sea of Japan and southern California.

SIZE: HB 1.42–2.13 m (4.7–7 ft); WT 43–272 kg (95–600 lb); males much larger than females.

FORM: males dark gray to brown, with reddish-brown underparts and flippers; mane short; females and immature males grayish-brown with reddish-brown underparts; pale area on chest.

DIET: fish, especially pollock and lanternfish; also squid in deeper waters.

BREEDING: only one pup born at a time, in summer, after a gestation of 3.5–4 months.

OTHER INFORMATION: lifespan about 25 years. Dives to depths of 207 m (679 ft). Active from dusk to dawn; sleeps by day while floating on one side.

CONSERVATION STATUS: not at risk, but numbers are declining sharply, most probably due to competition with commercial fisheries for food, and fatalities through drowning in fishing nets.

WALRUS

Odobenus rosmarus

Family: Odobenidae

THE WALRUS'S TUSKS MAY *measure 1 m (3.3 ft) in length. They are used in dominance conflicts. When basking in the sun, the skin turns deep pink, as blood runs closer to the surface to cool down.*

DISTRIBUTION: Arctic waters along the coasts of North America and Russia. Prefers shallow water near pack ice.

SIZE: HB 2.5–4.2 m (8.2–13.8 ft); WT 565–1,210 kg (1,246–2,668 lb); males larger than females; Pacific walruses are larger than those found in the Atlantic.

FORM: color ranges from pale-tawny to cinnamon-brown, darkest on chest and belly; immature animals darker; the Pacific walrus has a larger "beard" of sensory bristles than the Atlantic walrus.

DIET: bottom-dwelling invertebrates such as mussels, clams and starfish; also crustaceans, fish, seals and carrion.

BREEDING: only one young born at a time, in early summer, after a gestation of 15–16 months.

OTHER INFORMATION: lifespan up to 40 years.

CONSERVATION STATUS: not endangered, but numbers seriously reduced as a result of past hunting; still poached today for their ivory, increasingly since taking elephant ivory became illegal.

NORTHERN ELEPHANT SEAL

Mirounga angustirostris

Family: Phocidae

THE BULBOUS NOSE OF THE BULL ELEPHANT *seal can be inflated to act as an amplifier for its loud roars, which can be heard up to 1 km (0.6 mi) away.*

DISTRIBUTION: northwest Pacific Ocean; breeding beaches are located on offshore islands of the southwest USA and Mexico.

SIZE: HB 3–5 m (10–11.5 ft); wt 0.9–2.9 tonnes (0.9–2.9 tons); males much larger than females.

FORM: color dark gray. The necks of adult bulls are often heavily scarred from fighting.

DIET: deep-water and bottom-dwelling fish and squid.

BREEDING: only one pup born at a time, in winter, after a gestation of 11 months.

OTHER INFORMATION: lifespan up to 14 years in the wild, longer in captivity. The deepest-diving of the seals, reaching up to 894 m (2,934 ft). Can stay under water for almost 50 minutes. Once exploited for their blubber.

CONSERVATION STATUS: not threatened, but numbers reduced almost to extinction by overhunting during the last century. Genetic diversity now low, which may reduce the species' ability to adapt to change.

HOODED SEAL

Cystophora cristata

Family: Phocidae

DISTRIBUTION: north Atlantic and Arctic Oceans, usually in deep water near drifting ice, most commonly from northwest Canada and Greenland to Iceland and Svalbard, occasionally Alaska and Russia, and south to Florida and Portugal.

SIZE: HB 2.0–2.5 m (6.56–8.2 ft); WT 145–400 kg (320–882 lb); males slightly larger than females.

FORM: color bluish or silvery-gray, with irregular black or brown patches on back and sides, and smaller patches on neck and belly; face black to behind eyes. Has large claws on flippers, and wide nostrils. Young ("blue men") are bluish, with silvery bellies; spots develop with age.

DIET: mainly deep water fish, such as cod, halibut and Red perch.

THE HOODED SEAL HAS A LARGE, *fleshy proboscis, or bood, which hangs over the snout. In the male this can be inflated, and the air inside used to force a bright red balloon-like septum out through one nostril as a threat or mating display.*

BREEDING: only one young born at a time, in spring on the ice floes, after a gestation of almost a year.

OTHER INFORMATION: lifespan up to 35 years. Lives alone outside the breeding season. Females come onto the ice to give birth. Males remain nearby to guard their mates.

CONSERVATION STATUS: not threatened, but numbers were reduced by hunting earlier this century. Now only a little subsistence hunting occurs.

GRAY SEAL

Halichoerus grypus

Family: Phocidae

OUTSIDE THE BREEDING SEASON, THE GRAY SEAL WILL *wander far and wide. Young seals have been known to travel over 1,000 km (620 mi) in less than a month.*

DISTRIBUTION: 3 main populations in temperate and subarctic coastal waters: in northwest Atlantic Ocean from southern Greenland and Labrador south to Massachusetts; in northeast Atlantic from Svalbard (Norway) and Murmansk coast west to Ireland and southern Iceland; and a small group in the inner Baltic Sea.

SIZE: HB 1.8–2.3 m (5.9–7.5 ft); WT 86–310 kg (190–684 lb); male up to 3 times larger than female, with massive shoulders and a longer snout.

FORM: color gray, darker above, with black spots and blotches below; males often darker and more heavily spotted than females; newborn pups whitish.

DIET: cod, halibut, salmon, herring, lamprey; squid and octopus.

BREEDING: one pup born on the sea ice, after a gestation of 11.5 months.

OTHER INFORMATION: lifespan up to 46 years.

CONSERVATION STATUS: not at risk, but numbers are declining through persecution by fishermen for alleged taking of fish stocks, drowning in fishing tackle and pollution from oil spills. Young seals may drown in the wakes of ships.

56

AMAZON MANATEE

Trichechus inunguis

River manatee
Family: Trichechidae

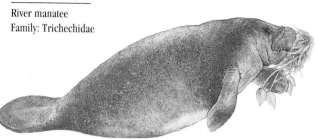

THE LAZY LIFESTYLE OF THE AMAZON MANATEE
requires little energy, so it can survive on a
low-nutrient diet of water plants. It has over
40 m (130 ft) of intestines to help it digest the
tough plant fibers.

DISTRIBUTION: throughout the
Amazon river system.

SIZE: HB 2.5–2.8 m (8.2–9.2 ft);
WT 350–500 kg (772–110 lb).

FORM: color gray, often with white or
pink patch on breast. Unlike other
manatee species, the skin is smooth,
and flippers have no nails. Skin covered
in sparse thin hairs; thick bristles on lips.

DIET: water plants.

BREEDING: only one young born at a
time, after a gestation of 12–14 months.
Weaned after about 2 years. Breeds only
every 2 or 3 years.

OTHER INFORMATION: lifespan over
12 years in captivity. The manatee has
very heavy bones to help it stay on the
river bed. Its lungs extend the length of
its body, helping to distribute buoyancy
evenly. To compensate for the wear on
its teeth caused by the tough plant
fibers, replacement teeth slowly move
forward from the back of the jaw, as in
elephants.

CONSERVATION STATUS: endangered by
overhunting (exacerbated by its slow
reproduction rate), drowning in fishing
nets, and pollution due to soil erosion
caused by deforestation and riverside
settlements.

57

RUFFED LEMUR

Varecia variegata

Family: Lemuridae

THE RUFFED LEMUR'S STRIKING COLORING IS IN FACT *a good camouflage against the bright light and dark shade of the forest. It feeds mainly at night, when its loud calls burst through the darkness.*

DISTRIBUTION: forests of northeastern Madagascar.

SIZE: HB 510–600 mm (20–23 in); TL 560–650 mm (22–25 in); WT 3.2 –5 kg (6.6–11 lb).

FORM: color shows variable patterning in black-and-white, red-and-white, or brown-and-white, which can differ on left and right sides of body. Fur long and soft, with a ruff from ears to chin.

DIET: leaves and fruit.

BREEDING: 1–3 young born at a time, in a nest of twigs and leaves, after a gestation of 90–102 days. It is the only lemur to leave its young in the nest.

OTHER INFORMATION: lifespan up to 19 years in captivity. Lives in small family groups. Feeds mainly at night; likes to sunbathe by day.

CONSERVATION STATUS: endangered as a result of loss of its forest habitat and hunting.

DWARF BUSH BABY

Galago demidovii

Dwarf or Demidoff's galago,
Demidoff's bush baby
Family: Lorisidae

THE DWARF BUSH BABY IS A
*nocturnal animal. Its large
eyes are adapted for night
vision; its big ears help it
to detect the movements
of insect prey
in the dark.*

DISTRIBUTION: dense tropical forests of Africa, especially among dense vines or lianas. 3 distinct populations: Senegal, southern Mali, Upper Volta and south-west Nigeria; Congo, Uganda, Burundi, Zaire and western Tanzania; a small group along the coast from southern Somalia to northern Tanzania.

SIZE: HB 105–155 mm (4–6 in); TL 150–215 mm (6–8 in); WT 46–120 g (1.6–4.2 oz).

FORM: color ranges from grayish-brown to bright ginger, with paler underparts.

DIET: mainly small insects; also fruits, tree sap and nectar.

BREEDING: only one young born at a time, after a gestation of 111–114 days.

OTHER INFORMATION: lifespan up to 12 years in captivity. Sleeps in hollow trees by day in groups of up to 30. Adapted to an arboreal life: its thumbs spread wide to provide a powerful grip on branches; its long tail acts as a bal-ancer while it leaps from tree to tree.

CONSERVATION STATUS: threatened by destruction of its forest habitat.

SLENDER LORIS

Loris tardigradus

Family: Lorisidae

DISTRIBUTION: forests of India and Sri Lanka.

SIZE: HB 175–264 mm (6.8–10 in); no external tail; WT 85–348 g (3–12 oz).

FORM: color gray or reddish; eyes surrounded by two black spots separated by narrow white line down to nose. Slender build.

DIET: mainly insects, but also shoots, fruits, small lizards, birds and bird eggs.

BREEDING: 1 or 2 young born at a time, after a gestation of 166–169 days.

THE SLENDER LORIS IS A SLOW-MOVING TREE-DWELLER. *Its opposable first digits and broad finger pads give it a powerful grip; it also has a particularly mobile hip joint for climbing.*

OTHER INFORMATION: lifespan up to 15 years in captivity. A solitary, nocturnal animal. When disturbed, it will "freeze" and remain motionless for hours. Its extremely slow movements enable it to get close to its prey before pouncing on it. The Slender loris and the related Slow loris seem to be able to eat food that would be toxic to most animals, such as millipedes and ants.

CONSERVATION STATUS: not at risk.

GOLDEN POTTO

Arctocebus calabarensis

Angwantibo
Family: Lorisidae

THE GOLDEN POTTO IS A QUIET, *nocturnal tree-dweller. If threatened, it rolls itself up into a ball with just its short tail sticking out. The hairs of its tail fan out and distract the attacker, giving the potto the chance of a quick bite.*

DISTRIBUTION: in the lower levels of tropical forests and scrubby plantations of central Africa, from Nigeria to Congo and Zaire.

SIZE: HB 229–305 mm (9–12 in); TL 10 mm (0.4 in); WT 150–500 g (5–18 oz).

FORM: coat long and woolly, light reddish to golden brown with a golden sheen, often with paler underparts; face darker, with a white line from forehead to nose; young have white spots. Index finger just a stub. More slender and light than the potto.

DIET: insects, especially caterpillars, and fruits.

BREEDING: only one young born at a time, after a gestation of 131–136 days.

OTHER INFORMATION: lifespan over 20 years in captivity. A solitary, nocturnal animal. Marks its territory with urine. An agile predator, it can rear up on its hind legs to capture insects in flight. Its highly opposable first digits give it a good grip on the branches.

CONSERVATION STATUS: threatened by loss of its forest habitat and by hunting.

SPECTRAL TARSIER

Tarsius spectrum

Sulawesi tarsier,
Celebes tarsier
Family: Tarsiidae

THE SPECTRAL TARSIER HAS HUGE *eyes for night vision and can turn its head through nearly 360 degrees to follow the movements of its prey.*

DISTRIBUTION: forests and scrub in southeast Asia, on the islands of Sulawesi, Sanghir, Peleng and Selajar.

SIZE: HB 130 mm (5 in); TL 220 mm (8.5 in); WT 120 g (4.2 oz).

FORM: coat silky; color ranges from buff to dark brown, with buff, gray or bluish-gray underparts. Tail naked except for a long tassel of hairs at tip. Eyes huge. Ears thin, membranous, almost naked.

DIET: mainly insects; also other small invertebrates, lizards, snakes, birds and bats.

BREEDING: only one young born at a time, after a gestation of 180 days.

OTHER INFORMATION: lifespan over 13 years in captivity. Lives in small family groups. Nocturnal; sleeps by day clinging to a tree trunk using its tail as a support. Large pads on its fingers and toes give it a good grip when climbing. Can leap up to 6 m (20 ft) by suddenly straightening its folded hind legs. The heel and foot bones are elongated and fused to help in leaping.

CONSERVATION STATUS: threatened by destruction of its forest habitat.

SADDLE-BACK TAMARIN

Sanguinus fuscicollis

Brown-headed tamarin
Family: Callitrichidae

TAMARINS ARE AT HOME AT ALL LEVELS OF THE *forest. They can climb and leap between the branches with ease, but will also hunt for insects and other prey on the ground. Their curved, pointed nails help them grip the bark.*

DISTRIBUTION: tropical forests and woodlands of upper Amazon region in southern Colombia, Ecuador, Peru and Brazil.

SIZE: HB 175−270 mm (7−10.5 in); TL 250−380 mm (10−16 in); WT 300 −380 g (10.6−13.4 oz).

FORM: color very variable, mainly dark brown with fine light brown or buff marbling on back, forming a sharply demarcated "saddle"; tail dark brownish-black; cheeks covered in white hairs. One subspecies is white all over. Forehead, crown and cheeks have long fur. Does not have a mustache, unlike some of its relatives.

DIET: insects, spiders, small lizards, young birds, bird eggs, shoots, fruits, nectar and flowers.

BREEDING: 1−2, rarely 3, young at a time after a gestation of 140−145 days.

OTHER INFORMATION: lifespan over 10 years. A good climber and acrobat, but dislikes water; populations separated by river systems have evolved into many different subspecies. Lives in small groups. Tamarins make good fathers, helping to rear young, assisting at the birth, caring for them between feeds, and washing and grooming them.

CONSERVATION STATUS: not at risk.

BLACK HOWLER MONKEY

Alouatta caraya

Family: Cebidae

BLACK HOWLER MONKEYS PROCLAIM THEIR PRESENCE *to neighboring troops at every opportunity. The expandable throat sac acts as a resonator and their cries can be heard up to 5 km (3 mi) away. The female is in the foreground.*

DISTRIBUTION: forests of South America, from Brazil to eastern Bolivia, Paraguay and northern Argentina.

SIZE: HB 500–650 mm (19.5–25 in); TL 545–650 mm (21–25 in); WT 7.5–7.6 kg (16.5–17 lb).

FORM: coat of male black, of female yellowish-brown. A large monkey with coarse hair, a naked face and heavy lower jaw, and a prehensile tail which is naked on underside for extra grip.

DIET: mainly leaves and fruits.

BREEDING: one young at a time, after a gestation of 180–194 days. Young rides on mother's back for almost one year.

OTHER INFORMATION: lives in troops of 3–19 individuals, with more females than males. Male has a large, wide-angled lower jaw and elastic throat sac to enable it to produce powerful cries.

CONSERVATION STATUS: at risk.

HUMBOLDT'S WOOLLY MONKEY

Lagothrix lagothrica

Brown woolly monkey
Family: Cebidae

LIKE MANY SOUTH AMERICAN MONKEYS, HUMBOLDT'S *woolly monkey uses its tail as an extra limb. Hanging by its tail leaves both its hands free to manipulate flowers and leaves or pluck fruits.*

DISTRIBUTION: forests of South America east of the Andes from Colombia to central Brazil.

SIZE: HB 390–580 mm (15–22.5 in); TL 560–730 mm (22–28.5 in); WT 5.5–6.5 kg (12–14 lb).

FORM: color ranges from gray to olive-brown, dark brown or black; head often darker, almost black. Head large and round; body heavy; tip of prehensile tail naked on underside for extra grip.

DIET: shoots, leaves, flowers, fruits, nuts, bark.

BREEDING: only one young born at a time, after a gestation of 225 days; breeds only every 1.5 to 2 years.

OTHER INFORMATION: lifespan over 25 years in captivity.

CONSERVATION STATUS: endangered by hunting for their meat; the young are often captured as pets, which may involve killing the mother; also at risk from habitat destruction.

65

Ateles geoffroyi

Geoffroy's
spider monkey
Family: Cebidae

THE BLACK-HANDED SPIDER
*monkey lives among the
small branches at the very
top of the forest. It swings
through the trees, using its
extremely long, flexible tail
rather like a rope.*

DISTRIBUTION: rainforests and mountain forests of Central America, from northeastern Mexico to western Panama.

SIZE: HB 340–520 mm (13–20 in); TL 590–840 mm (23–33 in); WT 7.5–7.6 kg (16.5–17 lb).

FORM: color ranges from golden-brown to red or dark brown; hands and feet black. Head relatively small. Thumb reduced to a stump: the monkey uses its finger and toes like a hook, from which to swing along branches.

DIET: leaves, shoots, fruits, seeds.

BREEDING: only one young born at a time, after a gestation of 210–225 days; thought to breed only every 3 years.

OTHER INFORMATION: lifespan over 30 years in captivity. The tail acts as a fifth limb and can support the whole body weight while hanging. It can also be used to pick up objects. On rare visits to the ground, may run on two legs.

CONSERVATION STATUS: threatened through habitat loss and hunting; some subspecies virtually extinct.

66

BROWN CAPUCHIN

Cebus apella

Black-capped, Hooded or Tufted capuchin
Family: Cebidae

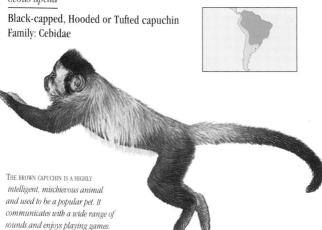

THE BROWN CAPUCHIN IS A HIGHLY
*intelligent, mischievous animal
and used to be a popular pet. It
communicates with a wide range of
sounds and enjoys playing games.*

DISTRIBUTION: moist forests of south America east of the Andes and north of Chile and Uruguay.

SIZE: HB 330–565 mm (13–22 in); TL 380–560 mm (15–22 in); WT 2.5–3.9 kg (5.5–8.6 lb).

FORM: color usually light to dark brown, with paler underparts; extremities of limbs black; facial pattern varies, but usually pale skin shows through on face, surrounded by black sideburns extending to chin; black cap forming a downward-pointing triangle on forehead, which may extend to form tufts each side of crown.

DIET: omnivorous, mainly fruits, berries, seeds and nuts, shoots, flowers, plant sap and bark; also insects and spiders, small vertebrates, eggs; sometimes crabs and other shellfish.

BREEDING: only one young born at a time, after a gestation of 153–161 days.

OTHER INFORMATION: lifespan over 44 years in captivity. Capuchins use their hands to manipulate objects.

CONSERVATION STATUS: not threatened, but certain subspecies in the Atlantic rainforest of eastern Brazil are endangered by deforestation and hunting.

NIGHT MONKEY

Aotus trivirgatus

Douroucouli, Owl monkey
Family: Cebidae

DISTRIBUTION: forests of Central and South America, from Panama to northern Argentina, except in French Guiana, Guyana, Uruguay, Chile and eastern Brazil.

SIZE: HB 240–475 mm (9.4–18.5 in); TL 220–420 mm (8.6–16.4 in); WT 0.8 –1.3 kg (1.8–2.9 lb).

FORM: color ranges from grizzled-brown to gray or reddish, with buff-white to bright orange underparts; head has white patches surrounding eyes, rising to a triangular point above.

DIET: mainly fruits, nuts, flowers, tree sap and leaves; also insects, small vertebrates and eggs.

THE NIGHT MONKEY IS THE ONLY TRULY NOCTURNAL *species of primate and has particularly large eyes. The markings on its face have led to its nickname of "owl monkey".*

BREEDING: only one young at a time, rarely 2, after a gestation of 150–153 days.

OTHER INFORMATION: lifespan over 13 years. Has very acute night vision and communicates by sound in the dark.

CONSERVATION STATUS: not at risk.

MANDRILL

Papio sphinx

Family: Cercopithecidae

THE MALE MANDRILL'S STRIKING *colors are used in displays to avoid physical conflict. When aroused, the colors become more intensive, and he thrashes his arms and "yawns" to show his large, fang-like teeth.*

DISTRIBUTION: dense rainforests of western Africa, in Cameroon, Equatorial Guinea, Congo and Gabon.

SIZE: HB 500–950 mm (19.5–37 in); TL 70–120 mm (3–5 in); WT 11–28 kg (24–62 lb).

FORM: color olive to brown, females duller. Adult male has yellow beard and neck; eyes ringed with black; brightly colored patches of bare skin on face, ribbed cheeks; bright blue to purplish-blue bridge; tip of nose scarlet; and pads of bare skin on buttocks pink to crimson, bluish at sides. Both sexes have beard and mane.

DIET: fruits, nuts, seeds, roots, leaves, mushrooms; also invertebrates and small vertebrates.

BREEDING: only one young at a time, after a gestation of 167–176 days.

OTHER INFORMATION: lifespan up to 46 years. Forages on the ground, turning over twigs and stones with its hands. Sleeps in trees. Lives in small groups led by a single adult male.

CONSERVATION STATUS: threatened by hunting for its meat, by deforestation and by international trade for zoos and research.

OLIVE BABOON

Papio anubis

Family: Cercopithecidae

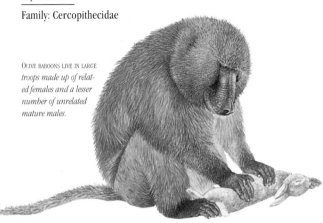

OLIVE BABOONS LIVE IN LARGE *troops made up of related females and a lesser number of unrelated mature males.*

DISTRIBUTION: open woodlands and grasslands of Africa south of the Sahara; also in several mountain areas in the Sahara.

SIZE: HB 500–950 mm (19.5–37 in); TL 380–600 mm (15–23 in); WT 15–30 kg (33–66 lb).

FORM: color dark olive-green, with black face; naked skin of buttocks violet-brown, turning pink during pregnancy.

DIET: eats almost anything, but especially grass, leaves, fruits, nuts, seeds, roots, tubers and flowers; also invertebrates, young birds and small mammals, including young gazelles.

BREEDING: one young born at a time, rarely twins, after a gestation of 173–193 days.

OTHER INFORMATION: lifespan up to 45 years. Sleeps in trees or on cliff ledges.

CONSERVATION STATUS: not at risk.

BARBARY APE

Macaca sylvanus

Barbary macaque
Family: Cercopithecidae

DISTRIBUTION: oak and cedar forests of the high Atlas mountains in Algeria and Morocco, and on Gibraltar. It is not known if the latter population is a natural relict, or descendants of introduced animals. It was originally found over much of Europe.

SIZE: HB 500–600 mm (19.5–23 in); tail absent; WT 11–15 kg (24–33 lb).

FORM: color yellowish-gray to grayish-brown, with paler underparts.

DIET: leaves, shoots, buds, bark, fruits, berries, seeds, roots; occasionally invertebrates.

BREEDING: only one young born at a time, rarely twins, after a gestation of about 7 months.

ONE OF THE FEW MONKEYS WITHOUT A TAIL, THE *Barbary ape is the only macaque living outside of Asia. Legend has it that when the last Barbary ape leaves the Gibraltar colony, British rule will end there.*

OTHER INFORMATION: lifespan over 20 years. An inquisitive animal, on Gibraltar it is known for picking tourists' pockets. Adult males will care for young, often two or more males interacting together with a youngster.

CONSERVATION STATUS: threatened by widespread loss of its forest habitat and by persecution for its raids on crops.

RHESUS MACAQUE

Macaca mulatta

Rhesus monkey
Family: Cercopithecidae

THE RHESUS MACAQUE IS A HIGHLY *adaptable animal, often found around human habitation, where it can be quite a nuisance, stealing food from shops and houses.*

DISTRIBUTION: from Afghanistan through India and Nepal to Indochina and southern China, in a wide range of habitats from sea level to about 2,500 m (8,205 ft).

SIZE: HB 450–640 mm (17.5–25 in); TL 190–320 mm (7.5–12.5 in); WT 5.5 –12 kg (12–26.5 lb); males slightly larger than females.

FORM: color brown with paler underparts; face and rump naked, red in adult. No swelling on rump.

DIET: shoots, fruits, seeds, roots, crops, bark and tree sap; small invertebrates.

BREEDING: only one young born at a time, rarely twins, after a gestation of 135–194 days; breeds only every 2 years.

OTHER INFORMATION: lifespan over 30 years. The so-called rhesus factor, found in human blood, was discovered in rhesus monkey blood in 1940. This species is common in zoos and is widely used in research.

CONSERVATION STATUS: not threatened, but export for research has reduced numbers in some areas.

GRAY-CHEEKED MANGABEY

Cercocebus albigena

Family: Cercopithecidae

THE GRAY-CHEEKED MANGABEY *lives in large groups that advertise their presence by loud, low-pitched calls, "whoop-gobbles", that carry a long way.*

DISTRIBUTION: forests of western and central Africa, from Cameroon to Uganda.

SIZE: HB 440–620 mm (17–24 in); TL 680–1,000 mm (26.5–39 in); WT 4–11 kg (8.8–24 lb).

FORM: fur soft and black, with brownish or grayish-brown fur on shoulders; cheeks grayish. A slender monkey with an oval head and rather long snout. Fingers and toes partly webbed.

DIET: feeds high in trees on fruits, nuts, seeds, shoots and flowers; also insects, other invertebrates and small vertebrates. Occasionally raids crops. Its powerful jaws and large incisors enable it to crack open nuts and seeds.

BREEDING: one young born at a time, after a gestation of about 170 days.

OTHER INFORMATION: lifespan over 30 years. Lives in mixed-sex groups of 6–30 individuals.

CONSERVATION STATUS: not at risk.

PATAS MONKEY

Erythrocebus patas

Red guenon, Military monkey, Hussar monkey
Family: Cercopithecidae

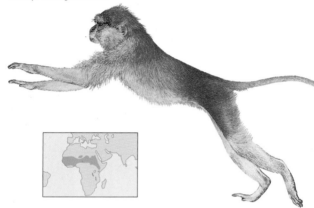

THE PATAS MONKEY FORAGES ON THE GROUND.
It lives in a habitat with little cover and relies on speed to escape danger. It has long limbs and can sprint at speeds of up to 55 km (33 mi) per hour.

DISTRIBUTION: grasslands and wood-land savanna of Africa, from Senegal and Ethiopia south to Kenya and Tanzania.

SIZE: HB 500–875 mm (19.5–34 in); TL 500–750 mm (19.5–29 in); WT 4–13 kg (9–29 lb); males much larger than females.

FORM: coat shaggy, reddish-brown; underparts, extremities and rump white; scrotum bright blue; penis red; face black with white mustache; cap brighter red, with black line from face to ear. Head rounded.

DIET: forages on the ground for fruits (especially acacia fruits), galls, leaves, crops and insects; also takes tree sap.

BREEDING: only one young born at a time, after a gestation of 176 days.

OTHER INFORMATION: lifespan over 21 years. Can stand up on hind legs to look around, using its tail for support.

CONSERVATION STATUS: not at risk.

74

PROBOSCIS MONKEY

Nasalis larvatus

Family: Cercopithecidae

DISTRIBUTION: mangrove swamps and lowland rainforests of Borneo, except in central Sarawak.

SIZE: HB 533–762 mm (21–30 in); TL 559–762 mm (22–30 in); WT 7–22.5 kg (15.5–50 lb); adult male about twice weight of female.

FORM: coat orange-white or pale orange, richer on lower chest, variably tinged with gray and flecked with black; shoulder and back tinged reddish; crown reddish-orange with frontal whorl and narrow nape extension flanked by paler cheek and chest ruff; triangular rump patch adjoining tail. Newborn has vivid blue facial skin. Adult male has elongated, tongue-shaped, pendulous nose. Proboscis monkeys have a thickset build.

THE MALE PROBOSCIS MONKEY'S *huge bulbous nose may be a means of attracting females, or it may help to dissipate excess body heat.*

DIET: mainly leaves, especially pedada leaves; also fruit and flowers.

BREEDING: one young born at a time, after a gestation of about 166 days.

OTHER INFORMATION: lifespan over 13 years in captivity. It is a good swimmer, and will dive in from a height of 16 m (52 ft) or more; it can also swim under water. The male's resonant honking call is much louder than the female's.

CONSERVATION STATUS: endangered by clear-cutting of its mangrove habitat.

KLOSS GIBBON

Hylobates klossii

Beeloh
Family: Hylobatidae

THE KLOSS GIBBON SWINGS THROUGH *the trees, using its hands as hooks and its long arms like a pendulum, a process called brachiation. The thumb is free almost to the wrist.*

DISTRIBUTION: confined to the Metawai islands off the Sumatran coast.

SIZE: HB 440–640 mm (17–25 in); no tail; WT 5–6 kg (11–13 lb).

FORM: color brownish-black to black, with white eyebrows; infant whitish. Slender, with short fur.

DIET: mainly fruits.

BREEDING: only one young born at a time, rarely twins, after a gestation of probably 7–7.5 months.

OTHER INFORMATION: lifespan probably over 24 years. Lives alone or in small family groups in a specific territory. Loud calls serve to prevent gibbons intruding on one another's territory.

CONSERVATION STATUS: endangered by loss of habitat to logging and agriculture, and by hunting for meat and for trade. Since it breeds only every 2 or 3 years, this is exacerbated.

COMMON CHIMPANZEE

Pan troglodytes

Family: Pongidae

THE COMMON CHIMPANZEE, *man's closest relative, has a complex social life. Gestures, displays and vocalizations are important in establishing the social ranking of an individual.*

DISTRIBUTION: west and central Africa, north of River Zaire, from Senegal to Uganda and Lake Tanganyika.

SIZE: HB 635–940 mm (25–37 in); no tail; height when erect 1.0–1.7 m (3.3–5.6 ft); WT 26–90 kg (57–20 lb); males larger than females.

FORM: color mainly black, but older animals may turn gray; most animals have a short white beard; face and skin of hands and soles of feet vary from pink to brown or black, usually becoming darker with age.

DIET: leaves, shoots, flowers, stems, fruits, seeds, tree sap, bark; also insects, honey, eggs and mammals, such as young deer, antelope and monkeys.

BREEDING: only one young born at a time, rarely twins, after a gestation of 225 days; breeds only every 3–6 years.

OTHER INFORMATION: lifespan over 50 years. Chimpanzees are famed for their use of tools, which may consist of modified twigs or other objects. Tools are used to extract termites from their nests, crack nuts and carry water.

CONSERVATION STATUS: threatened by loss of habitat, overhunting and persecution for the damage they do to crops.

ORANG-UTAN

Pongo pygmaeus

Family: Pongidae

THE ORANG-UTAN USES ITS ARMS
to swing through the trees.
An adult's arms may be over
2 m (6.6 ft) long, reaching
its ankles when erect.

DISTRIBUTION: once widespread in southeast Asia
and Indochina, now con-
fined to forests of northern Sumatra and most of
lowland Borneo.

SIZE: HB 1.25–1.5 m (4–5 ft); no tail;
height when sitting 0.7–0.9 m (2.3–
3 ft); WT 40–90 kg (88–198 lb); males
larger than females.

FORM: coat thin and shaggy, ranging
from bright orange in young animals
to maroon or dark chocolate in some
adults; face pinkish in young animals,
black in adults. Adults, especially old
males, have pronounced cheek pads.

DIET: mainly fruits, especially
wild figs; also young shoots, bark,
insects, bird eggs and small vertebrates.

BREEDING: only one young born at a
time, after a gestation of 233–265 days;
breeds only every 3 or 4 years.

OTHER INFORMATION: lifespan up to
60 years.

CONSERVATION STATUS: endangered
through habitat loss and past collection
for zoos and as pets.

GORILLA

Gorilla gorilla

Family: Pongidae

FOR ALL ITS POWERFUL *appearance, the gorilla is a peaceful vegetarian. It settles most of its disputes by letting off steam through displays of aggression and chest-beating.*

DISTRIBUTION:
3 main populations: the Mountain gorilla (*G. g. beringei*) in mountain forests of Zaire, Rwanda, Uganda, Cameroon and Gabon; the Western lowland gorilla (*G. g. gorilla*) in east-central Africa; and the Eastern lowland gorilla (*G. g. graueri*) in lowland Zaire.

SIZE: HB 1.5–1.8 m (4.9–5.9 ft); height when standing (stands with knees slightly bent) 1.25–1.75 m (4.1–5.7 ft); no tail; WT 70–275 kg (15–606 lb); males larger than females.

FORM: color black to brownish-gray, turning gray with age; older males ("silverbacks") develop a broad silvery-white saddle; skin jet black.

DIET: plant material, especially shoots, buds, stems and leaves.

BREEDING: only one young born at a time (if twins, usually only one survives), after a gestation of 250–270 days; breed only every 3.5–4.5 years.

OTHER INFORMATION: lifespan about 35 years in the wild, 50 in captivity.

CONSERVATION STATUS: Eastern lowland gorilla and Mountain gorilla highly endangered, due to past hunting, habitat destruction and civil wars.

AFRICAN ELEPHANT

Loxodonta africana

Family: Elephantidae

THE AFRICAN ELEPHANT IS THE WORLD'S LARGEST LAND *animal. The muscular trunk, made from the upper lip and nose, is used as a hand when feeding, a straw when drinking, a shower when bathing, and a snorkel when crossing deep rivers.*

DISTRIBUTION: Africa south of the Sahara.

SIZE: HB 6–7.5 m (20–25 ft); TL 1–1.3 m (3.3–4.3 ft); SH 1.6–2.7 m (5.3–8.9 ft); tusk length up to 3.5 m (13 ft); tusk weight up to 18 kg (40 lb); WT 2.4–6.3 tonnes (2.4–6.2 tons).

FORM: color grayish-black when young, becoming pinkish with age; skin only sparsely covered in coarse hairs. Tail tip flattened.

DIET: plants, mainly grasses, trees branches, bark and shrubs; may raid tourist camps and crops.

BREEDING: one young born at a time, rarely twins, after a gestation of 22 months. Breed only every 2.5–9 years.

OTHER INFORMATION: lifespan about 60 years in wild, over 80 in captivity.

CONSERVATION STATUS: threatened by habitat destruction and by poaching.

INDIAN ELEPHANT

Elephas maximus

Family: Elephantidae

DISTRIBUTION: forests and grasslands of Asia and Indochina, from the Indian subcontinent and Sri Lanka to Malaysia, Indonesia and southern China.

SIZE: HB 5.5–6.6 m (18–22 ft); TL 1.5–2.1 m (5–7 ft); SH 2.4–2.9 m (8–9.5 ft); WT 2.7–5.4 tonnes (2.7–5.3 tons).

FORM: skin dark gray to brown, often mottled around forehead, ears, base of trunk and chest with pinkish blotches.

DIET: mainly grasses, shoots, stems, leaves, vines and roots.

BREEDING: only one young born at a time, rarely twins, after a gestation of about 21–22 months.

AN INTELLIGENT, DOCILE ANIMAL, THE INDIAN *elephant has been trained for centuries to carry timber and humans. It feeds mainly at night, resting in the shade by day.*

OTHER INFORMATION: lifespan about 40 years in wild, up to 70 in captivity.

CONSERVATION STATUS: endangered by widespread habitat loss, especially deforestation, by hunting for its ivory and by persecution for its raids on the crops of local farmers. Rarely breeds in captivity

ROCK HYRAX

Procavia capensis

Dassie
Family: Procaviidae

THE ROCK HYRAX IS AN AGILE ROCK-CLIMBER AND IS *also at home in trees. Its feet have rubbery, sweaty soles with a good grip. It is a social animal and uses over 20 different sounds to communicate.*

DISTRIBUTION: rocky scrub areas of the Middle East, south Arabian Peninsula, and Africa.

SIZE: HB 305–550 mm (12–21 in); no external tail; SH 150–305 mm (6–12 in); WT 1.8–5.4 kg (4–12 lb).

FORM: fur short, dense and coarse, light to dark brown or brownish-gray, with creamy underparts.

DIET: mainly grass and leaves, including some plants that are poisonous to other animals. Obtains most of its water from its food.

BREEDING: 1–6 young born at a time, after a gestation of 202–245 days.

OTHER INFORMATION: lifespan at least 8.5 years in the wild, up to 11 in captivity. Its closest relatives are the hoofed mammals, or ungulates. Its gut contains symbiotic bacteria to help it break down tough plant fibers. It shelters in a rock crevice or makes a burrow. Feeds in small groups; one member of the group keeps a look-out for danger. In cool weather they huddle in groups.

CONSERVATION STATUS: not at risk.

AARDVARK

Orycteropus afer

Ant bear, Earth pig
Family: Orycteropodidae

THE AARDVARK IS ONE OF THE *world's fastest diggers: with its powerful claws, it can move earth faster than several men with shovels. It scrapes its way into termite mounds.*

DISTRIBUTION: Africa south of Sahara.

SIZE: HB 1.0–1.6 m (3.3–5.3 ft); TL 445–610 mm (17–24 in); SH 600–650 mm (23–25 in); WT 50–82 kg (110–181 lb).

FORM: color ranges from yellowish-gray to brownish-gray, often darker on legs and paler on head and tail; may appear reddish when stained by soil. Ears tubular; can be folded back to avoid dirt when burrowing.

DIET: mainly ants, termites and other insects.

BREEDING: only one young born at a time, in or just before the rainy season, after a gestation of about 7 months.

OTHER INFORMATION: lifespan up to 23 years in captivity. Adaptations for feeding include powerful, blunt claws for digging, tough skin and stiff whiskers on its snout and around its eyes to protect against bites and stings, and a long tongue (up to 30 cm/12 in) coated in sticky saliva to which the insects adhere.

CONSERVATION STATUS: threatened by habitat loss and by persecution.

PRZEWALSKI'S HORSE

Equus przewalskii or *Equus caballus*

Family: Equidae

DISTRIBUTION: steppes of Mongolia, near the Altai Mountains.

SIZE: HB 2.2–2.8 m (7.2–9.2 ft); TL 0.9–1.1 m (3–3.6 ft); SH 1.2–1.5 m (3.9–4.9 ft); WT 200–350 kg (441–772 lb).

FORM: color grayish-brown on back and flanks, yellowish-white on belly; mane and tail dark brown; inside of legs grayish. Smaller than most domestic horses, but heavily built with large head, short, stiff mane and long tail.

DIET: mainly grasses.

BREEDING: only one young born at a time, after a gestation of 340 days.

THE PROBABLE ANCESTOR OF THE DOMESTIC HORSE, *the small, sturdy Przewalski's horse resembles horses depicted in Paleolithic cave paintings, along with other hunted animals.*

OTHER INFORMATION: lifespan about 20 years.

CONSERVATION STATUS: endangered, almost extinct in the wild. Overhunted since the Stone Age; suffers competition with livestock for grazing and water; also as a distinct species at risk from interbreeding with domestic horses.

ASIATIC ASS

Equus hemionus

Onager, Kulan, Kiang, Dzeggetai
Family: Equidae

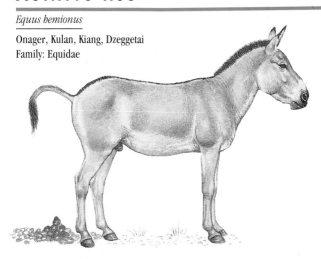

THE ASIATIC WILD ASS ROAMS LARGE AREAS IN SEARCH *of grazing in the desert and can go for long periods without water. It is known to interbreed with domestic horses.*

DISTRIBUTION: deserts and steppes of southern Mongolia, Turkmenistan, northern Iran, northwestern India and Pakistan.

SIZE: HB 2–2.5 m (6.6–8.2 ft); TL 300–400 mm (12–16 in); SH 1–1.4 m (3.3–4.6 ft); WT 200–290 kg (441–639 lb).

FORM: color reddish-brown to yellowish-brown, lighter in winter; prominent dark dorsal stripe that continues down tail; belly white.

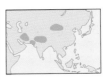

DIET: mainly grasses.

BREEDING: one young born at a time, after a gestation of 11–12 months.

OTHER INFORMATION: lifespan about 20 years.

CONSERVATION STATUS: threatened by overhunting, loss of habitat and by interbreeding.

GREVY'S ZEBRA

Equus grevyi

Family: Equidae

GREVY'S ZEBRA HAS BEEN HUNTED ALMOST TO *extinction for its beautiful coat. It is the largest of the zebras. Unlike most zebras, it forms only temporary social groups; others form large herds.*

DISTRIBUTION: deserts of east Africa, in Ethiopia, Somalia and northern Kenya.

SIZE: HB 2.5–3 m (8.2–9.8 ft); TL 380–600 mm (15–23 in); SH to 1.6 m (to 5.3 ft); WT 352–450 kg (776–993 lb).

FORM: coat has narrow vertical black-and-white stripes, curving across haunches to become horizontal on legs; belly white; mane may be brownish. Newborn foals are brown-and-black, and their manes extend along the back all the way to the tail.

DIET: grasses.

BREEDING: only one young born at a time, after a gestation of 12–13 months.

OTHER INFORMATION: lifespan about 20 years. Thought to be closely related to the ancestor of zebras.

CONSERVATION STATUS: endangered, as a result of past hunting and competition with domestic livestock.

MALAYAN TAPIR

Tapirus indicus

Asian tapir
Family: Tapiridae

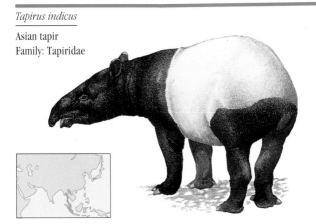

DISTRIBUTION: southeast Asia, from Burma and Thailand to Malaysia and Sumatra.

SIZE: HB 1.85–2.4 m (6–8 ft); TL 50–100 mm (2–4 in); SH 0.9–1.1 m (3–3.6 ft); WT 250–365 kg (551–805 lb).

FORM: color of head, shoulders, legs and tail black; rest of body white; very clear-cut color change divides body into black-white-black sandwich. Young are dark reddish-brown, with yellow and white stripes and spots. Snout and upper lips are elongated to form a short, muscular proboscis, which helps to manipulate food.

DIET: plant material.

THE MALAYAN TAPIR'S BOLD COLORATION IS ACTUALLY *a good camouflage in the moonlit jungle. The pattern helps to disguise the body outline in the deep undergrowth.*

BREEDING: only one young born at a time, rarely twins, after a gestation of 390–403 days.

OTHER INFORMATION: lifespan about 30 years. Communicates in the dark forest by shrill whistles and scents. Likes to wallow in mud. They are excellent swimmers and spend much time in water feeding and cooling off. If alarmed can remain submerged for several minutes.

CONSERVATION STATUS: endangered by destruction of its forest habitat.

87

INDIAN RHINOCEROS

Rhinoceros unicornis

Great Indian or Greater one-horned rhinoceros
Family: Rhinocerotidae

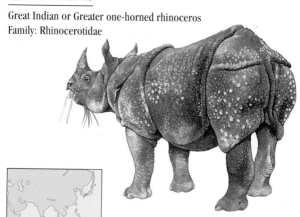

THE INDIAN RHINOCEROS'S HORN CAN BE UP TO *529 mm (21 in) long and is much sought after for use in eastern medicines. When feeding, the rhino wraps its prehensile upper lip around plants and tears them up.*

DISTRIBUTION: grasslands, swamps and cultivated areas of India (Assam), Nepal and Bhutan.

SIZE: HB 1.5–3.8 m (4.9–12.5 ft); TL 0.7–0.8 m (28–1.5 in); SH 1.5–1.9 m (4.9–6.2 ft); WT 1.6–2.2 tonnes (1.6–2.2 tons).

FORM: color gray, pinkish in folds. Skin almost naked, except fringes of bristles around ears and tip of tail; skin has loose folds arranged like a suit of armor, and is covered in knobs. Tail has tuft of hairs.

DIET: mainly grasses, reeds and twigs.

BREEDING: only one young at a time, after a gestation of 15–16 months; breeds only every 3 years.

OTHER INFORMATION: lifespan 40 years. Lives alone, but uses communal dung heaps. Communicates by sounds, and by scent from urine, feces and scent glands in the feet.

CONSERVATION STATUS: endangered; numbers reduced by past hunting are now being decimated by poaching; habitat is also being lost.

88

BLACK RHINOCEROS

Diceros bicornis

Hooked-lipped rhinoceros
Family: Rhinocerotidae

THE BLACK RHINO BROWSES ON *trees and shrubs, using its prehensile upper lip to pull down twigs. Mature bulls will fight, sometimes to the death, over access to the females.*

DISTRIBUTION: Africa from Somalia to the Cape.

SIZE: HB 2.9–3 m (9.5–9.8 ft); TL 600 mm (23 in); SH 1.6 m (5 ft); WT 950–1200 kg (2–2.6 tons).

FORM: color gray to brownish-gray or yellowish-brown. Upper lip protrudes in the middle and has prehensile tip. Has two horns, the front one the largest; rarely a third horn.

DIET: a browser rather than a grazer, feeding mainly on acacia leaves.

BREEDING: only one young born at a time, after a gestation of 15–16 months; breeds only every 3 years.

OTHER INFORMATION: lifespan 40 years. Rhinoceroses have acute senses of smell and hearing, but rather poor vision. Communication is by smell, trampling in its fresh dung to soak its feet with its distinctive smell. Scent serves to identify which individuals have passed along a particular path.

CONSERVATION STATUS: endangered by poaching of its horn for use in Oriental medicines and for carvings, especially Arab dagger handles.

WHITE RHINOCEROS

Ceratotherium simum

Square-lipped rhinoceros
Family: Rhinocerotidae

THE WHITE RHINO HAS
*the longest horn of
any rhino, often up
to 1.5 m (5 ft) long.
Highly prized for oriental
medicines, poaching has
brought it to the brink
of extinction.*

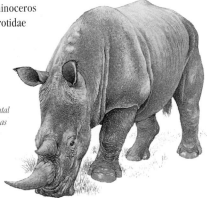

DISTRIBUTION: grasslands and open forests of southern and eastern Africa.

SIZE: HB 3.4–4 m (9.8–13 ft); TL 500–700 mm (19.5–27 in); SH 1.6–1.9 m (5.3–6.2 ft); WT 1.4–3.6 tonnes (1.4–3.5 tons); males larger.

FORM: color gray to brownish-gray or yellowish-brown. Skin naked except for fringes around ears and on tail. Upper lip square, not prehensile.

DIET: mainly grass.

BREEDING: only one young born at a time, after a gestation of about 16 months; breeds only every 2–4 years.

OTHER INFORMATION: lifespan 45 years. The characteristic square lip gives it a wide area of bite, which compensates for the shortness of the grasses it prefers to eat. Its short, thick legs and wide feet help to spread its great weight. Rhinos love to wallow in mud, which helps to cool them and to get rid of skin parasites.

CONSERVATION STATUS: endangered by hunting for its horn for use in Oriental medicines and carvings.

WILD BOAR

Sus scrofa

Wild pig
Family: Suidae

THE WILD BOAR IS PROBABLY THE ANCESTOR OF THE *domestic pig. It forages on the ground, pushing its snout through the soil in search of food. They forage in family groups, mostly in the daytime and at twilight.*

DISTRIBUTION: Europe, North Africa, Asia, Sumatra, Taiwan, Japan; introduced into many other regions.

SIZE: HB 0.9–1.8 m (3–5.9 ft); TL 300–400 mm (12–16 in); SH 0.55–1.1 m (1.8–2.2 ft); WT 44–320 kg (97–66 lb); males usually larger than females.

FORM: color brownish-gray; young striped giving good camouflage.

DIET: almost anything: grasses, herbs, fruits, berries, nuts, mushrooms; also insects, earthworms, grubs and small vertebrates such as mice, hares, birds, lizards, snakes, frogs and fish; eggs.

BREEDING: 1–2 young born at a time, after a gestation of 100–140 days.

OTHER INFORMATION: lifespan 21 years. Lives in large groups of up to 100 or more animals. Likes a mud bath to rid itself of skin parasites and to cool itself.

CONSERVATION STATUS: not at risk.

91

COLLARED PECCARY

Tayassu tajacu

Javelina, Javali, Baquiro, Chacharo
Family: Tayassuidae

DISTRIBUTION: forest, grassland and scrub of the Americas, from the south-western United States to northern Argentina.

SIZE: HB 800–980 mm (31–38 in); TL 45–55 mm (2 in); SH 300–475 mm (12–18.5 in); WT 17–25 kg (37–55 lb).

FORM: color grizzled gray with dark gray back; limbs blackish; whitish band runs diagonally from middle back to chest –the "collar".

DIET: grasses, leaves, fruits (especially cactus fruits), berries, nuts, seeds, roots, tubers, bulbs; small vertebrates such as mice, lizards, snakes, frogs; insects.

THE COLLARED PECCARY FINDS ITS FOOD MAINLY BY *smell; it has poor eyesight. It lives in groups of up to 50 animals. If attacked, a group of peccaries is capable of killing a predator as large as a puma.*

BREEDING: 1–4 young born at a time, after a gestation of 141–151 days.

OTHER INFORMATION: lifespan at least 24 years. The young are able to run and keep up with the group within a few hours of birth. If attacked, a few members of the group stand and face the attacker, while the rest make their escape; the outcome for a vigilant animal may be fatal.

CONSERVATION STATUS: not at risk.

HIPPOPOTAMUS

Hippopotamus amphibius

Family: Hippopotamidae

BULLS ARE TERRITORIAL AND HIGHLY AGGRESSIVE. *The hippopotamus spends most of the day resting in water in groups of up to 150 animals. Fights are usually ritualized, but males may fight to the death.*

DISTRIBUTION: rivers and lakes of west, central and east Africa.

SIZE: HB 2.9–5.1 m (9.5–16.7 ft); TL 350–560 mm (14–22 in); SH 1.4–1.7 m (4.6–5.6 ft); WT 1.4–4.5 tonnes (1.4–4.4 tons); males usually larger than females.

FORM: color grayish- or coppery-brown to blue-black; underparts pinkish. Skin almost naked. Exudes droplets containing a red pigment, appearing to "sweat blood". This secretion helps to regulate temperature.

DIET: mainly grasses.

BREEDING: only one young born at a time, after a gestation of 227–240 days.

OTHER INFORMATION: lifespan 40 years in the wild, 50 in captivity. Eyes and nostrils are raised above snout, so it can see and breath while almost totally submerged. Feeds at night, traveling up to 10 km (6 mi) inland.

CONSERVATION STATUS: not at risk, but populations are fragmented.

93

BACTRIAN CAMEL

Camelus bactrianus

Two-humped camel
Family: Camelidae

THE BACTRIAN CAMEL WAS DOMESTICATED AT LEAST *4,000 years ago. Invaluable as a beast of burden for carrying water and moving camp in desert areas, it is also a source of meat, milk, wool, hides and sinews. Its dried dung provides kindling and chemicals.*

DISTRIBUTION: deserts and dry steppes of the Gobi Desert in Mongolia and China. Domesticated animals found in most dry parts of the world.

SIZE: HB 2.3–3.5 m (7.5–11 ft); TL 350–550 mm (14–21 in); SH 1.8 –2.3 m (5.9–7.5 ft); WT 300–690 kg (662–1,521 lb).

FORM: color light to dark brown, darker in winter. Coat shaggy.

DIET: mainly grasses and herbs.

BREEDING: only one young born at a time, after a gestation of 12–14 months; breed only every 2 years.

OTHER INFORMATION: lifespan 40 years. Camels play a special role in rituals and customs of desert nomads.

CONSERVATION STATUS: endangered in the wild.

ARABIAN CAMEL

Camelus dromedarius

Dromedary, One-humped camel
Family: Camelidae

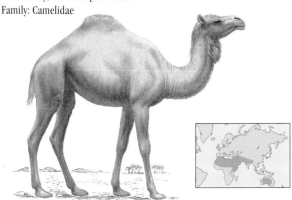

DISTRIBUTION: deserts and dry steppes of southwest Asia and north Africa; introduced into Australia

SIZE: HB 3 m (9.8 ft); TL 500 mm (19.5 in); SH 1.9–2.3 m (6.2–7.5 ft); WT 660–1,000 kg (1,455–2,205 lb).

FORM: color ranges from white to medium brown, sometimes with patches. Wool short, soft and fine.

DIET: grasses, herbs and shrubs.

BREEDING: only one young born at a time, after a gestation of 12–13 months. A dromedary produces up to 20 liters (42 US pints) of milk daily.

THE DROMEDARY CAN SURVIVE LOSING UP TO 40 PER cent of its body water. It can make up for this by drinking as much as 57 liters (120 US pints) of water at a time. Its hump stores fat, which breaks down to provide food.

OTHER INFORMATION: lifespan 40 years. The thicker wool over the hump insulates it from the heat of the sun. Long eyelashes and long hairs around the ears help to keep out sand. The nostrils can also be closed. Camels have a large gap between their front and back teeth, which is in the form of a hard pad on the upper jaw. This helps the tongue to mix saliva with the food to aid digestion.

CONSERVATION STATUS: not at risk.

LLAMA

Lama glama

Family: Camelidae

THE LLAMA WAS DOMESTICATED ABOUT 5,000 YEARS *ago and provides many useful products, including meat, woolen cloth, skin for sandals, hair for rope, fat for candles and dried droppings for fuel.*

DISTRIBUTION: dry, open country in the Andes mountains of central Peru, Bolivia, Chile and northern Argentina.

SIZE: HB 1.5–2.25 m (4.9–7.4 ft); TL 220–250 mm (8.6–9.8 in); SH 1–1.25 m (3.3–4.1 ft); WT 130–155 kg (130–342 lb).

FORM: color uniform or multi colored white, brown, gray or black, often blotched. Wool long, dense and fine, especially on back.

DIET: mainly grasses and leaves.

BREEDING: only one young born at a time, after a gestation of 11.5–12.5 months; breeds only every 2 years.

OTHER INFORMATION: lifespan 20 years. Related to the camels. Probably a domesticated form of the guanaco. The long legs enable it to travel long distances in search of grazing, while the long neck allows it to graze while standing. The soft underfur provides insulation against the cold, while the coarse guard hairs that overlie them protect against rain and snow.

CONSERVATION STATUS: not threatened. Existing animals probably all domesticated.

ALPACA

Lama pacos

Family: Camelidae

THE ALPACA IS BRED FOR ITS SOFT *wool, the finest of any animal. Unlike llama wool, alpaca wool grows continuously. It was once used to make the royal robes of the Incas.*

DISTRIBUTION: high altitude grasslands, alpine meadows and marshes of the Andes mountains from central Peru to western Bolivia.

SIZE: HB 1.2–2.25 m (3.9–7.4 ft); TL 150–250 mm (6–10 in); SH 0.94–1.04 m (3.1–3.4 ft); WT 55–65 kg (121–143 lb).

FORM: color ranges from uniform white, brown, gray or black to multicolored. A slightly smaller animal than the llama, with longer fur often reaching the ground and a shorter head. There is a tuft of hair on the forehead.

DIET: mainly grass.

BREEDING: only one young born at a time, after a gestation of about 11 months; breeds only every 2 years.

OTHER INFORMATION: lifespan 15 to 20 years. The alpaca has very sensitive feet and prefers soft marshy ground. Herds of several hundred roam free in the day and are corralled at night.

CONSERVATION STATUS: not at risk. Existing animals all domesticated.

MUSK DEER

Moschus spp

Family: Moschidae

DISTRIBUTION: forest and scrub of Asia, from eastern Afghanistan and Pakistan to China, the Himalaya, Siberia and Mongolia.

SIZE: HB 0.8–1.0 m (31–39 in); TL 40–60 mm (1.5–2.5 in); SH 500 –700 mm (20–28 in); WT 7–17 kg (15.5–37.5 lb).

FORM: color grayish-brown to golden, speckled; striped on the under part of neck. No antlers, but male has long, saber-like upper canine teeth that project well below the lips. The teeth can inflict deadly wounds when males fight.

DIET: mainly grass, shoots and moss, but also twigs and lichens.

THE YOUNG MUSK DEER PERSUADES ITS MOTHER TO *give it milk by touching her hind leg with its raised foreleg. This behavior is similar to the courtship behavior of other hoofed mammals.*

BREEDING: one or two young born at a time, after a gestation of 196–198 days.

OTHER INFORMATION: lifespan up to 20 years in captivity. The male secretes a brownish, wax-like substance – musk – from a gland in his abdomen. Musk is used in perfume, soap and medicines. Musk deer are often killed for their musk, but it can be extracted by hand during the breeding season; the deer are now reared on farms in China.

CONSERVATION STATUS: threatened by hunting and habitat loss.

REINDEER

Rangifer tarandus

Caribou
Family: Cervidae

THE REINDEER'S LARGE, SPREADING HOOVES HELP IT *to walk on marshy ground in summer and snow in winter. It migrates from the coniferous forest or mountain tundra in winter to the tundra in summer.*

DISTRIBUTION: Arctic and sub-arctic regions of Alaska, Canada, Greenland and adjacent islands, Scandinavia, Svalbard (Norway), Russia; introduced to South Georgia in the South Atlantic.

SIZE: HB 1.2–2.2 m (3.9–7.2 ft); TL 70 –210 mm (2.7–8.2 in); SH 0.9–1.4 m (3–4.6 ft); WT 60–318 kg (132–701 lb).

FORM: color brown in summer, gray in winter; white on rump, tail and above each hoof; males have white manes in the rut. Both sexes have antlers.

DIET: mainly leaves, herbs, sedges, lichens and fungi.

BREEDING: only one young born at a time, after a gestation of 227–229 days.

OTHER INFORMATION: lifespan 4–5 years in the wild, over 20 in captivity. Domesticated in Scandinavia and Russia.

CONSERVATION STATUS: threatened by hunting for its meat, skin and antlers.

WHITE-TAILED DEER

Odocoileus virginianus

Family: Cervidae

DISTRIBUTION: woodlands, forests and grasslands of North, Central and South America, from southern Canada to Peru and Brazil, excluding parts of the southwestern United States.

SIZE: HB 1.7–1.95 m (5.6–6.4 ft); TL 100–350 mm (3.9–14 in); SH 0.9–1.0 m (3–3.3 ft); WT 65–90 kg (143–198 lb); male larger than female.

FORM: color reddish-brown in summer, grayish-brown in winter; underparts, insides of thighs and underside of tail white; whitish patches on throat and insides of ears. Young spotted.

THE MALE WHITE-TAILED DEER SPORTS A FINE HEAD OF *antlers during the breeding season. Antlers are used to spar with other males for possession of the females.*

DIET: grasses, herbs, shoots, twigs, nuts and mushrooms.

BREEDING: one or two young born at a time, after a gestation of 204–205 days.

OTHER INFORMATION: lifespan up to 10 years in the wild, 16 in captivity. When fleeing from danger it raises its tail, exposing the bright white underside to alert other deer to the threat.

CONSERVATION STATUS: not at risk.

SIKA DEER

Cervus nippon

Japanese deer
Family: Cervidae

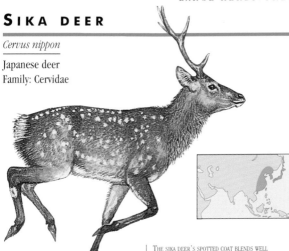

THE SIKA DEER'S SPOTTED COAT BLENDS WELL *with the dappled sunlight or moonlight of the forest. It is less sociable than most deer and is often found alone.*

DISTRIBUTION: forests, swamps and grasslands of the Far East, from south-eastern Siberia to Korea, Taiwan, northern Vietnam and Japan; introduced to parts of North America, Europe, Madagascar and New Zealand.

SIZE: HB 0.95–1.4 m (3.1–4.6 ft); TL 75–130 mm (3–5 in); SH 0.64–1.09 m (2.1–3.6 ft); WT 26–48 kg (57–106 lb); male larger than female.

FORM: color in summer chestnut-brown to yellowish-brown with white spots on sides and a white disk edged with black around tail; in winter grayish-brown with less obvious spots. Male has antlers during breeding season.

DIET: shoots, herbs, leaves, twigs and other plant material.

BREEDING: only one young born at a time in spring, after a gestation of about 217 days.

OTHER INFORMATION: feeds mainly between dusk and dawn. Uses at least 10 different sounds to communicate, ranging from soft whistles to loud screams.

CONSERVATION STATUS: endangered by overhunting for its meat and loss of its habitat to agriculture. Several subspecies are already extinct.

101

RED DEER

Cervus elaphus

Wapiti (N. America), Elk (N. America), Hangul, Shou, Bactrian deer
Family: Cervidae

A RED DEER STAG CALLS ("bells") during the rut. Stags try to intimidate each other by the power of their voices and by ritualized displays and fights.

DISTRIBUTION: forests, scrub, grasslands and mountains of North America, Europe, North Africa, Russia, Asia from Afghanistan to Kashmir, Tibet and southern Siberia; introduced to New Zealand, Australia and South America.

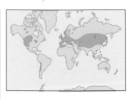

SIZE: HB 1.65–2.5 m (5.4–8.2 ft); TL 120–150 mm (4.7–5.9 in); SH 1.2 –1.5 m (3.9–4.9 ft); WT 70–220 kg (154–485 lb); male larger than female.

FORM: color red, brown or grayish-brown in summer, becoming darker and grayer in winter; rump patch yellowish, often with a dark tail stripe; young spotted.

DIET: grasses, herbs, buds, shoots, bark.

BREEDING: only one young born at a time, rarely twins, after a gestation of 235–265 days.

OTHER INFORMATION: lifespan up to 15 years in wild, over 26 in captivity.

CONSERVATION STATUS: certain subspecies are threatened by hunting and by loss of habitat, especially the Bactrian deer from Central Asia, the hangul from Kashmir and the shou from Tibet.

FALLOW DEER

Dama (Cervus) dama

Family: Cervidae

THE MALE FALLOW DEER HAS CHARACTERISTIC *branching antlers with broad tips and many points. It is a shy, secretive animal that usually stays in deep cover, feeding mainly between late afternoon and dawn.*

DISTRIBUTION: Europe from the British Isles to southern Sweden and western Russia, south to the Mediterranean, and Iran; introduced to many parts of the world. In the wild state are typically found in mature woodland.

SIZE: HB 1.3–1.75 m (4.3–5.7 ft); TL 150–230 mm (6–9 in); SH 0.8–1.05 m (2.6–3.4 ft); WT 30–100 kg (66–221 lb); male larger than female.

FORM: color very variable, typically fawn to white with white spots on back and flanks in summer, grayish-brown without spots in winter; underparts white; rump patch edged with black; black line down back and tail; white, black and intermediate forms common; young sometimes spotted. Males have large "palmate" antlers in breeding season.

DIET: grasses, herbs, shoots, buds, bark.

BREEDING: 1–3 young born at a time, in spring, after a gestation of 217–224 days (7 months).

OTHER INFORMATION: lifespan up to 25 years. Lives in single-sex groups.

CONSERVATION STATUS: not threatened; there are not many wild populations, but many captive ones. Numbers have declined due to past climate change.

WATER DEER

Hydropotes inermis

Family: Cervidae

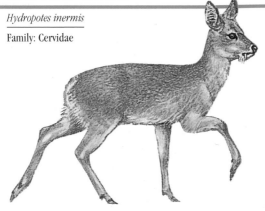

DISTRIBUTION: riversides, swamps and long grass in China and Korea; introduced to the UK.

SIZE: HB 0.75–1.0 m (2.5–3.3 ft); TL 60–75 mm (2.3–2.9 in); SH 450 –550 mm (17.5–21.5 in); WT 9–14 kg (20–31 lb); male larger than female.

FORM: color reddish-brown in summer, dull brown in winter; young have light spots. Antlers absent, but in both sexes the upper canine teeth form long, slightly curved tusks. The male's canines are up to 8 cm (3 in) long.

DIET: mainly grasses.

BREEDING: 1–2 young born at a time, after a gestation of 180–210 days.

THE TINY WATER DEER RELIES ON THE COVER OF LONG *reeds and grasses to conceal it from its enemies, but if threatened, it bounds away like a hare, arching its back as it leaps.*

OTHER INFORMATION: lifespan up to 12 years. The tusks are used as weapons and for intimidation: their threatening appearance is enhanced by black spots on the lower lip. Bucks mark territory by rubbing their foreheads on tree trunks, and by depositing scent on the ground from glands between the toes.

CONSERVATION STATUS: not at risk.

MOOSE

Alces alces

Elk (Europe)
Family: Cervidae

THE LARGEST DEER IN THE WORLD, A BULL MOOSE *stands up to 2.4 m (7.8 ft) high at the shoulder and his antlers may weigh 36 kg (19 lb). If fleeing from danger, it can easily outpace a fast-running horse on rough ground.*

DISTRIBUTION: marshlands and woodlands of North America from Alaska and Canada to Wyoming, northern Europe, Russia, Mongolia and China; introduced to New Zealand.

SIZE: HB 2.4–3.1 m (7.9–13.2 ft); TL 50–120 mm (1.9–4.7 in); SH 1.4–2.4 m (4.6–7.8 ft); WT 20–825 kg (44–1,819 lb); male larger than female.

FORM: color blackish-brown with paler brown underparts and lower legs; coat paler in winter. Nose very square.

DIET: mainly shoots and leaves of trees and shrubs, aquatic plants, twigs, bark.

BREEDING: 1 or 2 young born at a time, rarely 3, in spring, after a gestation of 240–250 days.

OTHER INFORMATION: lifespan up to 27 years. In summer visits salt licks and feeds on water plants.

CONSERVATION STATUS: not at risk.

REEVE'S MUNTJAC

Muntiacus reevesi

Chinese muntjac
Family: Cervidae

DISTRIBUTION: forests and other dense vegetation in China and Taiwan; introduced into southern England.

SIZE: HB 900 mm (3 ft); TL about 86–160 cm (3–6 in); SH 410 mm (16.4 in); WT 11–16 kg (24–35 lb).

FORM: color ranges from dark brown to yellowish- or grayish-brown with cream or white markings. Males grow short antlers in breeding season. Male's upper canine teeth form strongly curving teeth which project out of the mouth. Females have small bony knobs and tufts of hair in place of antlers.

DIET: grasses, bamboo shoots, leaves, fallen fruits, bird eggs, carrion.

THE MALE MUNTJAC HAS RATHER SMALL, STRAIGHT *antlers. He uses his saber-like tusks for fighting and defense. If he detects a predator nearby, he will make a deep barking sound to alert other deer and warn off the enemy.*

BREEDING: 1 or 2 young born at a time, after a gestation of 209–220 days.

OTHER INFORMATION: lifespan over 17 years in captivity. Unsociable; lives on its own and defends a territory, which it marks with scent from glands under the eyes to signal its presence to neighboring muntjacs. Are capable of hunting and killing small vertebrates by attacking with forelegs and tusks.

CONSERVATION STATUS: not at risk.

GIRAFFE

Giraffa camelopardalis

Family: Giraffidae

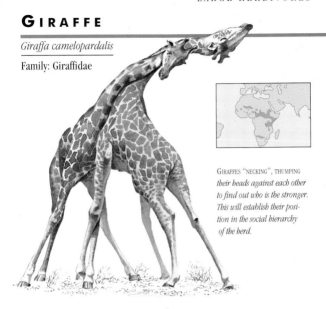

GIRAFFES "NECKING", THUMPING *their heads against each other to find out who is the stronger. This will establish their position in the social hierarchy of the herd.*

DISTRIBUTION: grasslands and open woodland in Africa south of the Sahara.

SIZE: HB 3.8–4.7 m (12.5–15.5 ft); TL 0.8–1.0 m (2.6–3.3 ft); SH 3.9–5.8 m (12.8–19.0 ft); WT 0.55–1.9 tonnes (0.54–1.87 tons).

FORM: coat patterned with orange-brown, russet or blackish patches on a cream or buff background; gets darker with age; underparts pale and unpatterned. Long neck has short mane.

DIET: mainly shoots and leaves of trees and shrubs, especially acacias.

BREEDING: only one young born at a time, rarely twins, after a gestation of 450–465 days.

OTHER INFORMATION: lifespan up to 25 years in the wild, 28 in captivity. Its height and excellent eyesight enable it to see for long distances above the vegetation. Although it has long legs, its maximum speed is only about 56 km (35 mi) per hour, but it has considerable stamina.

CONSERVATION STATUS: not threatened, but numbers and range are declining, especially small populations.

PRONGHORN

Antilocapra americana

Pronghorn antelope
Family: Antilocapridae

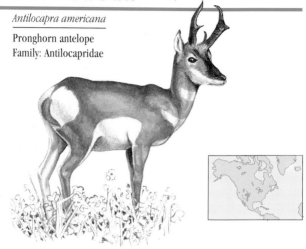

DISTRIBUTION: grasslands, scrublands and deserts of Canada, the western United States and part of Mexico.

SIZE: HB 1.0–1.5 m (3.3–4.9 ft); TL 75–100 mm (2.9–3.9 in); SH 0.8 –1.0 m (2.63–3.3 ft); WT 36–70 kg (79–154 lb).

FORM: color tan, sharply demarcated from white belly and lower flanks; white shield and crescent on throat; rump white; inner sides of limbs white; mature males have a black face mask and black glandular spot below the ear.

DIET: mainly grasses, herbs, leaves of small shrubs and cacti.

THE FASTEST LONG DISTANCE RUNNER IN THE WORLD, *the pronghorn can keep up a speed of 56 km (35 mi) per hour for 6 km (3.7 mi) and 88.5 km (55 mi) per hour for almost 1 km (0.62 mi). It travels in a series of long leaps, each covering 3 to 6 m (9.8–19.7 ft).*

BREEDING: 1–2 young born at a time, rarely 3, in spring, after a gestation of 250–252 days.

OTHER INFORMATION: lifespan up to 10 years in the wild, 12 in captivity.

CONSERVATION STATUS: not threatened, but the subspecies found in the Sonoran Desert and Baja California are endangered, mainly by loss of habitat to ranchers.

WATER BUFFALO

Bubalus bubalis

Asian water buffalo
Family: Bovidae

THE WATER BUFFALO IS RENOWNED FOR ITS BAD *temper. It likes to wallow in mud; this cools it and covers its body with a hard cake of mud that keeps irritating insects at bay.*

DISTRIBUTION: wild Water buffalo occur only in swampy parts of India; domesticated and feral animals are found in Asia, North Africa, Europe and South America.

SIZE: HB 2.4–3.0 m (7.8–9.8 ft); TL 0.6–1.0 m (2.0–3.3 ft); SH 1.5–1.9 m (4.9–6.2 ft); WT 0.7–1.2 tonnes (0.7–1.2 tons).

FORM: color slate-gray to black; domestic animals may be a mixture of black or brown and white. Both sexes have broad, almost horizontal horns with a spread of up to 2 m (6.6 ft).

DIET: aquatic and swamp vegetation.

BREEDING: only one calf born at a time, after a gestation of 300–340 days (10–11 months).

OTHER INFORMATION: lifespan up to 25 years in the wild, 29 in captivity.

CONSERVATION STATUS: endangered in the wild by habitat loss to agriculture, hunting for their meat, competition and interbreeding with domestic live-stock, and disease spread by livestock.

AMERICAN BISON

Bison bison

Bison, American buffalo
Family: Bovidae

HUNDREDS OF THOUSANDS
*of bison once roamed
the North American prairies,
yet by early last century
European settlers had hunted
them almost to extinction – only
a few hundred survived.*

DISTRIBUTION: prairies and other grasslands, open woodlands and mountains of North America. Now mainly confined to reserves.

SIZE: HB 2.1–3.5 m (6.9–11.5 ft); TL 300–600 mm (11.7–23.5 in); SH 1.5 –2.0 m (4.9–6.6 ft); WT 350–1,000 kg (772–2,205 lb); male larger than the female.

FORM: color reddish-brown to dark brown; often a beard on chin; males have a dark mane; calves reddish-brown. Both sexes have short curved horns. Female has thinner neck and horns and smaller hump than male.

DIET: mainly grasses and herbs; also mosses and lichens in winter.

BREEDING: one young born in spring, after a gestation of 270–300 days.

OTHER INFORMATION: lifespan up to 25 years. Bison can run at up to 60 km (37 mi) per hour and are also good swimmers.

CONSERVATION STATUS: the Plains bison subspecies was hunted almost to extinction in the last century, but is now recovering; the Wood bison is endangered and confined to a single national park.

COMMON DUIKER

Sylvicapra grimmia

Gray duiker, Bush duiker, Grimm's duiker
Family: Bovidae

A COMMON DUIKER "DUIKING" (FLEEING); NAMED *after the Afrikaans for a diver, it will dive into dense cover when threatened. Duikers like high-quality vegetation and will invade gardens to feast on vegetables and flowers.*

DISTRIBUTION: grasslands and mountains of Africa from Senegal and Ethiopia south to South Africa.

SIZE: HB 0.7–1.15 m (2.3–3.8 ft); TL 75–195 mm (2.9–7.6 in); SH 450 –700 mm (17.6–27.3 in); WT 12– 25 kg (26–55 lb); female usually larger than male.

FORM: color sandy to tan; dark stripe from nose to forehead. Ears rounded; males have slender horns with sharp points, ribbed at roots; females sometimes have small stunted horns.

DIET: browses trees and shrubs; also roots, tubers, bulbs and crops; occasionally termites, ants, snails, eggs, birds and small mammals.

BREEDING: only one young born at a time, rarely twins, after a gestation of about 210 days.

OTHER INFORMATION: lifespan over 14 years in captivity. Lives alone or in pairs. Active mainly at night.

CONSERVATION STATUS: not at risk.

KOB

Kobus kob

Family: Bovidae

A KOB ABOUT TO APPROACH A *female, using the characteristic head-high approach of courtship. Next, he will stroke her with his foreleg, before mating. Each buck defends a display territory, which the females will visit.*

DISTRIBUTION: savanna and other African grasslands, from Senegal to Kenya.

SIZE: HB 1.25–1.8 m (4.1–5.9 ft); TL 200–400 mm (7.9–15.8 in); SH 0.7 –1.05 m (2.3–3.4 ft); WT 50–120 kg (110–265 lb); male larger than female; males have horns up to 1 m (3.3 ft) long.

FORM: color variable, reddish-brown to yellowish-brown or ocher, often with whitish underparts; some subspecies, such as the Uganda kob shown here, have various white markings. Horns long, lyre-shaped, with spiral grooves.

DIET: grasses and herbs.

BREEDING: only one young born at a time, after a gestation of about 274 days (9 months).

OTHER INFORMATION: lifespan up to 17 years in captivity. In some populations, the males use a communal display area (lek) during the breeding season, in which each has its own small territory. Bucks proclaim their territory by loud whistles. Lives in large herds, sometimes containing several thousand animals.

CONSERVATION STATUS: not at risk.

112

GEMSBOK

Oryx gazella

South African oryx, Oryx gazelle
Family: Bovidae

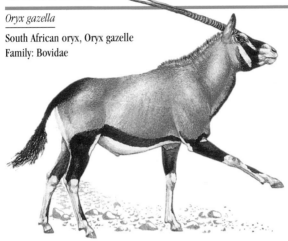

A MALE GEMSBOK ABOUT TO KICK A FEMALE WITH *his foreleg in a ritualized courtship display. The gemsbok's long legs help it travel up to 90 km (56 mi) a day in search of grazing.*

DISTRIBUTION: scattered populations in dry grasslands and deserts of southern and eastern Africa.

SIZE: HB 1.8–2.35 m (5.9–7.7 ft); TL 800–900 mm (31–35 in); SH 1.15–1.4 m (3.8–4.6 ft); WT 180–225 kg (397–496 lb). Both sexes have horns.

FORM: color fawn with white underparts; black face mask with white stripes on either side of eye; nose and chin white; black band down throat, across flanks, down upper part of front legs and outer side of upper hind legs; tail black.

DIET: mainly grasses and herbs.

BREEDING: one young born at a time, after a gestation of about 240 days.

OTHER INFORMATION: lifespan up to 20 years.

CONSERVATION STATUS: not at risk.

TOPI

Damaliscus lunatus

Tsessebe, Sassaby, Tiangs damalisc,
Korrigum, Bastard hartebeest
Family: Bovidae

A MALE TOPI APPROACHES A FEMALE, USING THE
*gesture typical of courting antelopes: head
up, ears laid back and tail held out.*

DISTRIBUTION: grasslands of Africa
from Senegal south to South Africa.

SIZE: HB 1.5–2.05 m (5–6.8 ft);
TL 400–600 mm (1.3–2 ft); SH 1.0–
1.3 m (3.3–4.3 ft); WT 120–200 kg
(165–352 lb).

FORM: color deep reddish-brown; front
of face, upper legs and tail tip black;
rest of legs yellowish-brown. Both sexes
have curved, ridged horns.

DIET: mainly grasses and herbs.

BREEDING: only one young born at a
time, after a gestation of 213–243 days.

OTHER INFORMATION: lifespan over
21 years in captivity. Can run at over
70 km (43.5 mi) per hour.

CONSERVATION STATUS: threatened by
overhunting, loss of habitat to agriculture and competition with domestic
livestock for grazing and water.

BRINDLED GNU

Connochaetes taurinus

Blue wildebeest, Blue gnu,
White-bearded wildebeest
Family: Bovidae

THE BRINDLED GNU LIVES IN LARGE
herds that may migrate long dis-
tances over the plains in search
of grazing and water. Males
assert dominance in pushing
matches using their horns.

DISTRIBUTION: grasslands of Africa, from Kenya to northern South Africa.

SIZE: HB 1.7–2.4 m (5.6–8 ft); TL 0.6 –1.0 m (2–3.3 ft); SH 1.15–1.45 m (3.8–4.8 ft); WT 140–290 kg (308– 638 lb); male larger than female.

FORM: color grayish-silver to slate-gray or dark gray, with brownish bands on neck, shoulders and front of body; tail black; tufts of long black hair hang from snout, throat and chest; black upright mane on neck; tail has long tuft. Both sexes have cattle-like horns.

DIET: mainly grasses; some herbs and shrubs.

BREEDING: only one young born at a time, after a gestation of 243–274 days.

OTHER INFORMATION: lifespan over 21 years in captivity. A newborn gnu can stand within 15 minutes of birth and can travel with the herd almost imme- diately. This is essential, because gnu rely on cooperative defense to protect them from predators.

CONSERVATION STATUS: not threat- ened, but numbers are decreasing. This is mainly as a result of competition with, and disease from, domestic live- stock; loss of habitat to ranching; and interruption of migration routes by fencing, which denies access to water.

BEIRA

Dorcatragus megalotis

Family: Bovidae

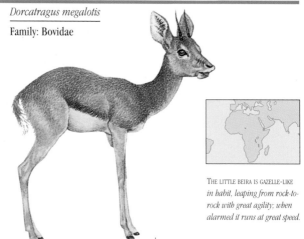

The little beira is gazelle-like *in habit, leaping from rock-to-rock with great agility; when alarmed it runs at great speed.*

DISTRIBUTION: stony hills and hot, dry plateaus with bushes in eastern Ethiopia, Djibouti and northern Somalia, bordering Red Sea and Gulf of Aden.

SIZE: HB 0.76–0.87 m (2.5–2.85 ft); TL 14–20 cm (5.5–7.9 in); SH 52–65 cm (20.5–26 in); WT 15–26 kg (33–57 lb).

FORM: color reddish-gray; upperparts finely speckled; underparts white; distinct dark line from shoulder to flank; head yellowish-red; legs fawn; tail white; white band around eyes. Horns only in males, curving slightly forward, up to 102 mm (4 in) long. Ears very large, marked inside with white hairs. Tail short and bushy. Legs long, with padded hooves. Muzzle pointed.

DIET: coarse grass and leaves of mimosas, from which it derives most of its water.

BREEDING: not known.

OTHER INFORMATION: forms small herds of 4 to 7 individuals, including 1 or 2 males, which feed in mornings and afternoons, resting in the middle of the day.

CONSERVATION STATUS: vulnerable; the beira has always been uncommon and its range has declined recently.

SPRINGBOK

Antidorcas marsupialis

Springbok
Family: Bovidae

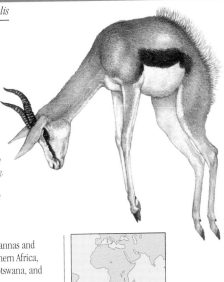

A SPRINGBOK "PRONKING":
leaping up to 3.5 m
(11.5 ft) into the air with
legs held stiffly vertical.
This behavior has given rise
to its name. While pronking,
it erects the white hairs on
the rump patch, a warning
signal to others.

DISTRIBUTION: dry savannas and other grassland of southern Africa, in Angola, Namibia, Botswana, and South Africa.

SIZE: HB 1.2–1.5 m (3.9–4.9 ft); TL 200–320 mm (7.8–12 in); SH 680 –900 mm (26.5–35 in); WT 20–30 kg (44–66 lb).

FORM: color bright reddish-brown with white underparts, separated by dark side band; face white with dark band from eye to snout; rump patch white; fold of skin along lower back and rump has line of white erectile hairs.

DIET: mainly grasses and herbs, leaves, roots, bulbs.

BREEDING: one young born at a time, after a gestation of about 168 days.

OTHER INFORMATION: lifespan up to 19 years in captivity. Springbok once migrated across the African plains in herds of over a million animals. After centuries of hunting and persecution for the damage such herds do to crops, numbers are much reduced, with herds seldom numbering more than 1,500.

CONSERVATION STATUS: not at risk.

117

BLACKBUCK

Antilope cervicapra

Indian blackbuck
Family: Bovidae

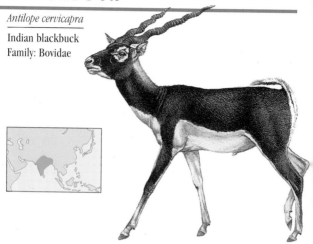

DISTRIBUTION: grassy plains and dry deciduous forests of India, with small populations in Nepal and on the Pakistan border. Large introduced populations in Argentina and Texas.

SIZE: HB 1.0–1.5 m (3.3–5 ft); TL 100–170 mm (4–6.8 in); SH 600–850 mm (2–2.8 ft); WT 25–35 kg (55–77 lb); male larger than female.

FORM: male dark brown on back, flanks and outside of legs, becoming darker with age; female yellowish-buff; both sexes have white underparts and insides of legs, and a white circle around the eye. Males have spiraling horns up to 685 mm (27 in) long.

A MALE BLACKBUCK IN A TERRITORIAL DISPLAY *posture. If this does not deter rivals, the black-buck will fight, lowering their heads and interlocking horns, pushing and twisting.*

DIET: short grasses, herbs, leaves, buds, fruits, cereals.

BREEDING: only one young born at a time, after a gestation of about 180 days (6 months).

OTHER INFORMATION: lifespan over 18 years. Leap into the air when alarmed.

CONSERVATION STATUS: not threatened, but numbers greatly reduced as a result of hunting for meat and sport, and loss of habitat to agriculture.

THOMSON'S GAZELLE

Gazella thomsoni

Family: Bovidae

THE THOMSON'S GAZELLE *relies on flight to escape from predators such as lions. It can reach speeds up to 80 km (50 mi) per hour, and zigzags to and fro, making it difficult for a heavier animal to keep up.*

DISTRIBUTION: savannas and other grasslands of east Africa, in Tanzania and Kenya, and a small population in southern Sudan.

SIZE: HB 0.8–1.1 m (2.6–3.6 ft); TL 190–270 mm (7.4–10.5 in); SH 550–650 mm (21.5–25.4 in); WT 15–30 kg (33–66 lb).

FORM: color bright fawn; underparts, inner sides of legs and front of neck white; dark band on flanks; broad bright fawn stripe down center of face; blackish stripes from eyes to snout; white circle around eye; inner sides of ear black with white border. Horns long, only slightly curved.

DIET: mainly grasses, herbs and leaves.

BREEDING: only one young born at a time, after a gestation of 160–180 days.

OTHER INFORMATION: lifespan over 10 years. Males hold small territories, which they defend fiercely, often engaging in up to 30 fights a day; fights involve clashing horns and pushing.

CONSERVATION STATUS: not at risk.

119

MUSK OX

Ovibos moschatus

Family: Bovidae

THE MUSK OX IS NAMED FOR THE *odor given off by males during the breeding season. The ox's large spreading hooves help to prevent it sinking into snow in winter and soft ground in summer.*

DISTRIBUTION: mountain and Arctic tundra of Northern America, from Alaska to Greenland; reintroduced to the Taymyr Peninsula, Russia.

SIZE: HB 1.9–2.45 m (6.2–8 ft); TL 90–140 mm (3.5–5.5 in); SH 1.2–1.51 m (3.9–5 ft); WT 180–410 kg (397–904 lb); male larger than female. Both sexes have broad horns that curve downward and outward.

FORM: color dark brown to black with light saddle and legs.

DIET: mainly grasses, sedges, herbs and shrubs.

BREEDING: only one young born at a time, rarely twins, in spring, after a gestation of 8–9 months.

OTHER INFORMATION: lifespan up to 24 years. The Musk ox's thick coat has long outer guard hairs resistant to rain and snow. The soft, dense under-fur traps air to insulate the ox from the cold. When threatened, Musk oxen form a circle with their heads and massive horns facing the enemy, and the young safely in the center.

CONSERVATION STATUS: not at risk.

MOUNTAIN GOAT

Oreamnos americanus

Rocky Mountain goat
Family: Bovidae

THE MOUNTAIN GOAT IS AT HOME ON
steep cliffs and mountainsides.
An expert climber and jumper,
its hooves have a hard, sharp
rim that can grip rock and ice.

DISTRIBUTION: high mountains of North America, from Alaska and Yukon to Oregon, Idaho and Montana; introduced into other parts of the region.

SIZE: HB 1.41–1.54 m (4.6–5 ft); TL 100–200 mm (3.9–7.8 in); SH 0.9–1.2 m (3–4 ft); WT 46–140 kg (100–310 lb); males considerably larger than females.

FORM: color yellowish-white. Long hair over shoulders and middle of neck forms a ridge or hump. Beard on chin. Horns short, sharply curved.

DIET: grasses, herbs, leaves, shoots, buds, fungi, lichens.

BREEDING: 1–3 young born at a time, in early summer, after a gestation of about 186 days. Young can follow their mother within a week.

OTHER INFORMATION: lifespan up to 18 years. Has a thin skull and does not indulge in head-to-head fights. Attacks involve jabbing at flanks and belly with the sharp horns, producing wounds that can be fatal. After giving birth, females become very aggressive, keeping males away from their young. In winter, females and young occupy the cliff areas, where grass is accessible.

CONSERVATION STATUS: not at risk, but some populations overhunted.

BARBARY SHEEP

Ammotragus lervia

Aoudad
Family: Bovidae

THE BARBARY SHEEP LIVES IN ROCKY COUNTRY WITH *very little vegetation, and relies on camouflage to avoid predators. If danger threatens, it remains motionless, relying on its coloration to conceal it.*

DISTRIBUTION: desert and semi-desert uplands (up to 3,900 m/12,200 ft) of North Africa, from Morocco and western Sahara to Egypt and Sudan. Introduced to Texas, New Mexico and California for sport-hunting.

SIZE: HB 1.3–1.65 m (4.3–5.4 ft); TL 150–250 mm (5.9–9.8 in); SH 0.75–1.12 m (2.3–3.7 ft); WT 40–145 kg (88–320 lb); male larger than female.

FORM: color reddish-tawny, with whitish insides of legs, chin, insides of ears and line on underparts. Long mane on throat, chest and upper part of forelegs. Both sexes have horns, those of males strongly curving.

DIET: grasses, herbs, shrubs, acacia leaves, lichens.

BREEDING: only one young born at a time, rarely twins, after a gestation of 154–161 days.

OTHER INFORMATION: lifespan up to 10 years in the wild, 20 in captivity. Rams do battle to collect females. Rival rams will face each other, then walk forward, accelerating into a run, then lowering their heads and ramming each other. Or they may lock horns and try to pull each other to the ground.

CONSERVATION STATUS: threatened in the wild by overhunting.

IBEX

Capra ibex

Family: Bovidae

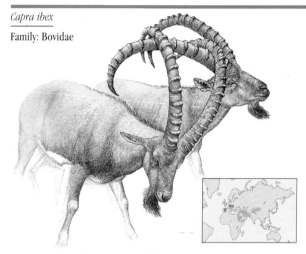

DISTRIBUTION: mountains and rocky deserts of Europe, the Middle East, North Africa, Asia east to Mongolia and China, usually above treeline up to 6,700 m (21,990 ft).

SIZE: HB 0.75–1.7 m (2.5–5.6 ft); TL 150–290 mm (5.9–11.3 in); SH 700–940 mm (27–37 in); WT 40–120 kg (88–265 lb); male considerably larger than female.

FORM: color brown; tail darker; underparts often paler in female; small white rump patch under tail; thick woolly beard. Horns of male scimitar-shaped, up to 1.4 m (4.6 ft) long; females thinner, up to 380 mm (15 in) long.

IBEX ARE SURE-FOOTED MOUNTAIN GOATS THAT CAN *climb almost vertical rock faces by jumping so quickly from rock to rock that they do not stay still long enough to overbalance.*

DIET: grasses and herbs.

BREEDING: only one young born at a time, rarely 2 or 3, in early summer, after a gestation of 150–180 days.

OTHER INFORMATION: lifespan up to 14 years. Males fight for rank and females by rearing up on hind legs and smashing heads together.

CONSERVATION STATUS: not threatened, but numbers are decreasing.

123

PYGMY TREE SHREW

Tupaia minor
Family: Tupaiidae

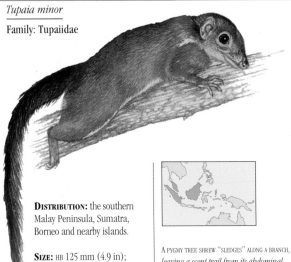

DISTRIBUTION: the southern Malay Peninsula, Sumatra, Borneo and nearby islands.

SIZE: HB 125 mm (4.9 in); TL 145 mm (5.7 in); WT 45 g (1.6 oz).

FORM: color olive, with off-white underparts. Tail long and bushy; snout short; claws poorly developed.

DIET: fruits, seeds, invertebrates, small vertebrates.

BREEDING: 1–4 young born at a time, after a gestation of 40–55 days. Shows very little parental care. Mother visits young only rarely to suckle. She recognizes them by scent she rubs on them; if this is lost, she may eat them. Sexually mature at about 2 months, so

A PYGMY TREE SHREW "SLEDGES" ALONG A BRANCH, *leaving a scent trail from its abdominal gland. Tree shrews have been classified as primates or insectivores, but recent evidence suggests they are very similar to the earliest placental mammals.*

populations can increase rapidly. Probably produce more than one litter a year.

OTHER INFORMATION: lifespan up to 10 years in captivity. Lives mainly in the trees, and its eyes are set well forward for good stereoscopic vision. Catches food with its snout rather than its paws. Nests in a tree hollow.

CONSERVATION STATUS: not at risk.

MALAYAN COLUGO

Cynocephalus variegatus

Malayan flying lemur
Family: Cynocephalidae

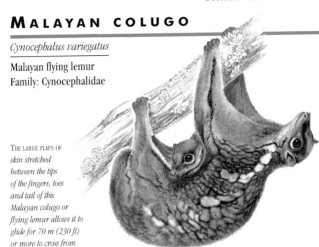

THE LARGE FLAPS OF *skin stretched between the tips of the fingers, toes and tail of this Malayan colugo or flying lemur allows it to glide for 70 m (230 ft) or more to cross from tree to tree.*

DISTRIBUTION: forests and plantations of Thailand, Indochina, southern China, Malaysia, and the islands of Java, Sumatra and Borneo.

SIZE: HB 340–420 mm (13.3–16.4 in); TL 220–270 mm (8.6–10.5 in); "wing-span" 700 mm (27.3 in); WT 1–1.8 kg (2.2–4 lb); female slightly larger than male.

FORM: upper surface of the flight membrane mottled grayish-brown with white spots; underparts paler; females tend to be more gray, males more brown or reddish.

DIET: leaves (young and mature), shoots, buds, flowers and soft fruits.

BREEDING: one young born at a time, rarely twins, after a gestation of about 60 days. The flight membrane can be folded near the tail to form a soft warm pouch for carrying the young.

OTHER INFORMATION: lifespan over 17 years in captivity. Spots and mottling of coat help to camouflage it on tree trunks flecked with sunshine. Has large eyes for nocturnal vision.

CONSERVATION STATUS: not at risk.

EUROPEAN BEAVER

Castor fiber

Eurasian beaver
Family: Castoridae

THE EUROPEAN BEAVER
landscapes its sur-
roundings, felling
trees to dam rivers
and create ponds in
which to build its
"lodges" of sticks and
mud. It has very large
front teeth (incisors)
for gnawing wood
and bark.

DISTRIBUTION: originally near ponds, rivers and lakes throughout forested regions from northwestern Europe and northern Asia to Japan. Now only scattered populations remain.

SIZE: HB 0.8–1.1 m (2.6–3.6 ft); TL 300–340 mm (11.7–13.3 in); SH 300–350 mm (11.7–13.7 in); WT 17–31.7 kg (37.5–69.9 lb).

FORM: color yellowish-brown to rich brown, with tawny to brown underparts; feet and tail black.

DIET: grasses, herbs, algae, herbs; in winter, twigs and bark.

BREEDING: 1–5 young born, in spring, after about 100–110 days gestation.

OTHER INFORMATION: lifespan up to 10 years in the wild, 35 in captivity. Lodge extends under water; underwater entrances provide access when the pond is frozen in winter. Sleeps a lot in winter, but emerges from time to time to feed from underwater caches of food.

CONSERVATION STATUS: not at risk, but numbers reduced as a result of overhunting in the last century for its pelt, and more recently by drainage of wetlands for agriculture and pasture, water pollution, and damming of waterways.

SOUTHERN FLYING SQUIRREL

Glaucomys volans

Family: Sciuridae

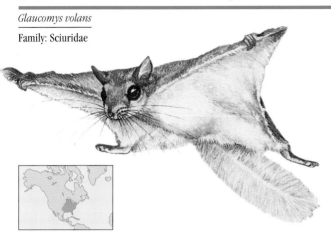

DISTRIBUTION: forests and woodlands of North and Central America, from southeastern Canada to the eastern United States and south to Honduras.

SIZE: HB 120–140 mm (4.7–5.5 in); TL 80–120 mm (3.1–4.7 in); WT 50–85 g (1.8–3 oz); female largest.

FORM: color gray on back, head and tail, sometimes tinged with brown; underparts white.

DIET: fruits, nuts, berries, bark, fungi, lichens.

BREEDING: 2–7 young born at a time, in spring and late summer, after 40 days gestation; often has 2 litters a year.

THE SOUTHERN FLYING SQUIRREL CAN GLIDE FOR UP TO *40 m (130 ft) between trees, using flaps of skin spread between its fingers and toes as a parachute. This flight membrane is supported and extended by rods of cartilage attached to the wrists.*

OTHER INFORMATION: lifespan over 17 years in captivity. The ability to glide between trees enables it to escape from arboreal predators, and also saves time and energy when switching trees. The squirrel can change direction in mid-flight by moving its arms or legs and by changing the angle of its tail. The underside of the flight membrane is very soft, to minimize friction, and its shape works like a crude airfoil.

CONSERVATION STATUS: not at risk.

SIBERIAN CHIPMUNK

Eutamias sibiricus (Tamias sibiricus)

Family: Sciuridae

THE SIBERIAN CHIPMUNK IS THE ONLY CHIPMUNK *found in the Old World. It has large cheek pouches that reach to its shoulders. It uses them to carry seeds and nuts to a special underground larder, where it may store up to 8 kg (18 lb) of food for use in winter.*

DISTRIBUTION: forests of Siberia, Mongolia, northern and central China, Korea and northern Japan.

SIZE: HB 120–170 mm (4.7–6.6 in); TL 80–115 mm (3.1–4.5 in); WT 50–120 g (1.8–4.2 oz).

FORM: color whitish-yellow to sandy-yellow, with white underparts; four light and five dark longitudinal stripes run along back; white stripe above and below each eye; tail light brown in center, with broad black lines on either side and narrow, white edges; overall color grayer in winter.

DIET: mainly dry food such as nuts and seeds; also buds, fruits, bulbs, mushrooms, insects and bird eggs.

BREEDING: 3–7 young born at a time, after a gestation of 31–45 days.

OTHER INFORMATION: the tricolored tail is used as a "follow-me" signal. Lives in a complex underground tunnel system or "lodge", with many winding tunnels. Sleeps for up to 5 months in winter, but wakes at regular intervals, so not true hibernation.

CONSERVATION STATUS: not at risk.

AMERICAN RED SQUIRREL

Tamiasciurus hudsonicus

Family: Sciuridae

THE AMERICAN RED SQUIRREL LOVES TO BURY FOOD *for use later. This habit is important in the recovery of forests after logging and other disturbances, as it helps to disperse seeds.*

DISTRIBUTION: North America, from Alaska and Canada to the western and northeastern United States and Appalachian Mountains.

SIZE: HB 165–230 mm (6.4–12 in); TL 90–160 mm (3.5–6.2 in); WT 140 –310 g (4.9–10.9 oz).

FORM: color in summer olive-brown, with blackish line on sides and rusty band along back; grayer in winter.

DIET: nuts, seeds, berries, buds, bark, fruits, sap, mushrooms, bird eggs.

BREEDING: 3–7 young born at a time, after a gestation of 33–35 days.

OTHER INFORMATION: lifespan about 10 years.

CONSERVATION STATUS: not at risk.

Xerus erythropus

Striped ground squirrel
Family: Sciuridae

THIS GEOFFROY'S GROUND SQUIRREL HAS ARCHED AND *fluffed its tail, a sign of anxiety. Typical of animals that dig underground burrows, their claws are long.*

DISTRIBUTION: north and northeast Africa, from southwestern Morocco and Senegal to eastern Sudan and south-western Kenya.

SIZE: HB 220–460 mm (8.6–17.9 in); TL 180–270 mm (7–10.5 in); WT 500–950 g (17.7–33.5 oz).

FORM: color yellowish-gray to reddish or brownish, with buff or whitish under-parts; bold white stripe on each flank; sometimes a stripe down center of back.

DIET: leaves, nuts, seeds, fruits, roots, tubers, bulbs, insects, eggs.

BREEDING: 2–6 young born at a time, after an unknown gestation period.

OTHER INFORMATION: lifespan up to 6 years in captivity. Live in open country in colonial burrows like those of prairie dogs. Can often be seen during the day standing up on hind legs looking around, scolding intruders or sun-bathing. When alarmed by predators they dash with a jumping gait to their burrows.

CONSERVATION STATUS: not at risk.

ALPINE MARMOT

Marmota marmota

Family: Sciuridae

AN ALPINE MARMOT SITTING ON ITS *haunches has spotted danger and is whistling a warning to others in the vicinity. They will dive into their burrows and hide.*

DISTRIBUTION: alpine meadows, pastures and forest edges of the Alps, Carpathians and Tatra Mountains of Europe.

SIZE: HB 420–540 mm (16.8–21.6 in); TL 165–175 mm (6.6–7 in); WT 2.3–5.7 kg (5.2–12.6 lb), heaviest in autumn; male larger than female.

FORM: color variable, from light yellowish-brown to red or dark gray, with paler underparts; white bridge on nose.

DIET: grasses, herbs (including some poisonous ones), leaves and flowers.

BREEDING: 1–7 young born at a time, after a gestation of 33–34 days.

OTHER INFORMATION: lifespan up to 15 years. Lives in a complex burrow system with several entrances, which provide bolt holes from hawks and eagles while feeding on the surface. In winter, they hibernate in the deepest chambers, perhaps 7 m (23 ft) below ground, when they live off their fat, which may comprise 20% of body weight. Chambers are lined with dried grass for insulation.

CONSERVATION STATUS: not threatened, but numbers have declined as a result of loss of habitat to agriculture.

PLAINS POCKET GOPHER

Geomys bursarius

Family: Geomyidae

DISTRIBUTION: open country of North America, from southern Manitoba and Wisconsin to eastern Kansas and Illinois.

SIZE: HB 130–240 mm (5.1–9.4 in); TL 50–120 mm (2–4.7 in); WT 300–450 g (10.6–15.9 oz); male twice as large as female.

FORM: color pale to dark brown, with paler underparts. Front paws have large curved digits with powerful curved claws for digging.

DIET: underground plant parts (roots, tubers, bulbs); some above-ground plants, such as leaves and shoots.

A PLAINS POCKET GOPHER RETURNS FROM A FORAGING *trip above ground with its cheek pouches full. Pocket gophers spend most of their time deep underground, in a series of feeding tunnels out of sight of predators.*

BREEDING: 1–8 young born at a time, after a gestation of 18–19 days.

OTHER INFORMATION: lifespan 4 years in the wild, over 7 in captivity. Lives in large burrow systems with a series of feeding tunnels and, deeper still, nesting chambers lined with soft grass, plus food storage chambers. While these tunnels may damage root crops, they also break up and aerate the soil.

CONSERVATION STATUS: not at risk.

GREAT CANE RAT

Thryonomys swinderianus

Family: Thryonomyidae

THE GREAT CANE RAT IS A PEST OF SUGAR *cane fields and cereal crops. It cuts runways in the long grass from its shelter to its favorite feeding places, and forages mainly at night.*

DISTRIBUTION: marshes and reedbeds of Africa, from Gambia and southern Sudan south to Namibia and South Africa.

SIZE: HB 430–580 mm (16.8–22.6 in); TL 170–260 mm (6.6–10.1 in); WT 4.5–8.8 kg (9.9–19.4 lb).

FORM: color speckled grayish-brown or yellowish-brown, with whitish or grayish underparts; tail brown above and buff below.

DIET: soft stems and grass roots, fallen fruits, nuts, cereal crops.

BREEDING: 1–6 young born at a time, after a gestation of 137–172 days; may have 2 litters a year. Makes a special nursery nest lined with grass and leaves.

OTHER INFORMATION: widely hunted for its meat. Lives in small groups. Home consists of abandoned burrows of porcupines or aardvarks, termite mounds, rock crevices or shallow burrows of its own making. Males fight for dominance by means of nose-to-nose pushing matches, each rat trying to knock the other over. Keeps its teeth sharp by gnawing on bones.

CONSERVATION STATUS: not at risk and is often regarded as a pest.

MERRIAM'S KANGAROO RAT

Dipodomys merriami

Family: Heteromyidae

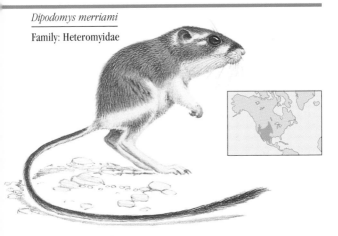

DISTRIBUTION: dry grasslands and semi-deserts of the southwestern United States, Baja California and northern Mexico.

SIZE: HB 100–200 mm (3.9–7.8 in); TL 100–125 mm (3.9–4.9 in); WT 35–180 g (1.2–6.4 oz).

FORM: color pale sandy-yellow or grayish-brown, with white underparts; tail long. Hind legs much longer and more powerful than forelegs.

DIET: mainly seeds; also leaves, buds, fruits, insects.

BREEDING: 1–6 young born, after a gestation of 28–32 days; breed up to 3

MERRIAM'S KANGAROO RAT HOPS ACROSS THE DESERT *like a miniature kangaroo, using its long tail as a balancer. Its large eyes and whiskers plus acute hearing are adaptations to a nocturnal life.*

times a year. Breeding success and numbers fluctuate with the availability of seeds, which is related to the occurrence and duration of winter rain.

OTHER INFORMATION: lifespan up to 5.5 years. Lives in a shallow underground burrow system with nesting and storage chambers. It plugs the entrance with soil, so that moist air from its breathing accumulates and prevents the rat dehydrating.

CONSERVATION STATUS: not at risk.

WOOD RAT

Neotoma sp.

Pack rat
Family: Muridae

DISTRIBUTION: prairies, dry grasslands, dry woodlands, mountains and swamps of southern United States and Mexico.

SIZE: HB 190–230 mm (7.4–9 in); TL 140–200 mm (5.5–7.8 in); WT 140–380 g (4.9–13.4 oz).

FORM: color pale grayish-fawn to dark gray or reddish-buff, with white, pale gray or buff underparts.

DIET: seeds, cacti, leaves, fruits. Gets much of its water from succulent cacti.

BREEDING: 1–7 young born at a time, after gestation of about 35 days.

OTHER INFORMATION: lifespan about 3 years. A wood rat house has several

A WOOD RAT OR PACK RAT CARRIES A BONE HOME. *Some wood rats build elaborate houses of twigs, bones, rocks and other material, including human debris like can tops, glass and trinkets, often stolen from campers.*

entrances, nesting chambers lined with grass, shredded bark and feathers, and a chamber for storing food. Sometimes feeding trails leading from the house are protected by walls of twigs. The house may be added to generation after generation and some are up to 2 m (6.6 ft) tall. A few species build dens in trees instead. Males will fight for females in the breeding season.

CONSERVATION STATUS: most species not threatened, but a few subspecies are at risk from habitat destruction.

SOUTH AMERICAN WATER RAT

Nectomys sp.

Neotropical water rat
Family: Muridae

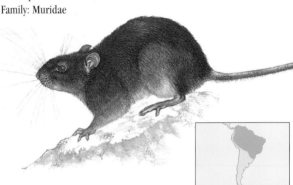

DISTRIBUTION: near lakes, streams and swamps in evergreen forests of northern and central South America and Trinidad.

SIZE: HB 160–250 mm (6.2–9.75 in); TL 165–250 mm (6.4–9.75 in); WT 160–420 g (6.5–14.8 oz).

FORM: color ranges from buff to tawny, speckled with brown, with paler flanks and whitish or grayish underparts, often tinged reddish-orange on chest. Hind feet large and powerful, with webbed toes that provide the main thrust when swimming; underside of tail and unwebbed parts of toes fringed with stiff bristles, which are also aids for swimming.

A SOUTH AMERICAN WATER RAT FORAGES MAINLY AT *night. Its large eyes and very long whiskers help it to find its way in the dark. It is a fast swimmer and climber; it usually seizes its prey with its forepaws.*

DIET: fruits, seeds, mushrooms and invertebrates (especially snails), tadpoles and small fish.

BREEDING: 2–7 young born at a time, after an unknown gestation period.

OTHER INFORMATION: makes nest in dense vegetation or under logs, roots or brushwood, or in decaying tree stumps. Often pursues its prey under water where it is a strong swimmer.

CONSERVATION STATUS: not at risk.

HARVEST MOUSE

Micromys minutus

Old World harvest mouse,
Eurasian pygmy mouse
Family: Muridae

DISTRIBUTION: grasslands, meadows, fields, thickets and reed beds of Europe, Russia and Asia, from western Europe eastwards to Siberia, Korea, China, Taiwan and Japan.

SIZE: HB 55–75 mm (2.1–2.9 in); TL 50–75 mm (2–2.9 in); WT 5–7 g (0.18–0.25 oz).

FORM: color yellowish-brown to reddish- or rusty-brown, with white or buff underparts; juveniles grayish. Tail long, used for balancing, as an anchor, and as a brake when climbing down plant stems.

DIET: buds, fruits, seeds, insects.

THE TINY HARVEST MOUSE BUILDS A NEST OF WOVEN grass blades. This turns pale brown with age, providing good camouflage against the ripening wheat stalks. This mouse is an agile climber; the outer toe on each hind foot is opposed like a thumb for gripping stems.

BREEDING: 1–13 young born at a time, in spring and summer, after a gestation of 17–18-days. Breed rapidly: young are born naked and helpless, but within 5 days they have fur; after 2 weeks or so they will leave the nest.

OTHER INFORMATION: lifespan up to 1.5 years in the wild, almost 5 in captivity. Range diminishing.

CONSERVATION STATUS: not at risk.

HOUSE MOUSE

Mus musculus

Family: Muridae

THE HOUSE MOUSE'S GREAT *adaptability has enabled it to spread around the world wherever man has settled. Where conditions are to its liking, it can produce up to 14 litters of 3–12 young a year, a potential of 168 young each year.*

DISTRIBUTION: original distribution probably from western Europe to Asia, now worldwide wherever there is human habitation. Tolerates a wide range of environmental conditions.

SIZE: HB 70–92 mm (2.7–3.6 in); TL 70–92 mm (2.7–3.6 in); WT 10–41 g (0.35–1.45 oz).

FORM: color brownish-gray with slightly paler underparts.

DIET: leaves, shoots, seeds (including stored cereal grains), roots, insects and other invertebrates, and almost any kind of human refuse, including glue, soap and paper.

BREEDING: 3–12 young born at a time, after a gestation of 19–21 days; up to 14 litters a year.

OTHER INFORMATION: lifespan up to 6 years in captivity. Associated with humans from prehistoric times, it would have benefited from the development of agriculture, in particular cereal crops. Houses provide it with shelter in winter and a generous supply of scraps and household waste. Modern varieties of pet mouse, coming in many color forms, are derived from this species. In bred strains are used in laboratory research.

CONSERVATION STATUS: not at risk.

BROWN RAT

Rattus norvegicus

Norway rat, Common rat
Family: Muridae

A SERIOUS PEST OF CEREAL CROPS, GRAIN *stores and cities, the Brown rat also carries several diseases, and parasites that carry diseases, such as bubonic plague and typhus, which can be lethal to humans.*

DISTRIBUTION: originally from the steppes of Asia, Mongolia, northern China and southern Siberia, it is now found near human habitation in many parts of the world, where it often displaces native rats.

SIZE: HB 180–260 mm (7.2–10.4 in); TL 150–220 mm (6–8.8 in); WT 140–400 g (5–14 oz).

FORM: color grayish-brown with paler belly; heavier than Black rat, with tail shorter than body.

DIET: almost anything, especially seeds (including cereal grains), nuts, fruits, vegetables, insects, small birds, fish, eggs, household waste, including soap, leather and paper.

BREEDING: 2–22 young born at a time, after a gestation of 21–26 days; may have up to 12 litters a year.

OTHER INFORMATION: lifespan several years. Lives in large packs with well-structured social hierarchies. In the wild, it excavates an underground burrow system with several entrances, branching tunnels, plus separate chambers for sleeping and food storage. Packs defend a living territory about 150 m (492 ft) in diameter.

CONSERVATION STATUS: not at risk.

MUSKRAT

Ondatra zibethicus

Family: Muridae

A MUSKRAT SITS ATOP ITS HOUSE TO *feed. It builds a mound-like house of grass and reeds plastered with mud. Up to 1 m (3.3 ft) high, the house contains a dry nest and several underwater exits.*

DISTRIBUTION: rivers, streams, lakes and marshes of North America, from Canada and Alaska south to northern Baja California; introduced to Europe and Asia.

SIZE: HB 229–325 mm (8.9–12.7 in); TL 180–295 mm (7.0–11.5 in); WT 0.6–1.8 kg (1.3–4 lb).

FORM: color ranges from silvery-brown to black, usually with slightly paler underparts; feet and tail dark brown to black. Has partly webbed feet fringed with bristles and a flattened tail.

DIET: leaves and shoots, especially cattails, bulrushes and grass; also invertebrates such as mussels and crabs, plus small fish.

BREEDING: 1–11 young born, after 25–30 days gestation; up to 6 litters a year.

OTHER INFORMATION: lifespan about 3 years in the wild, up to 10 in captivity. Active mainly at night. Gets its name from the musky odor with which it marks its territory. Can swim up to 100 m (330 ft) and stay underwater for up to 17 minutes. Calls using an abrupt whistle.

CONSERVATION STATUS: not at risk.

NORWAY LEMMING

Lemmus lemmus

Family: Muridae

DISTRIBUTION: tundra and moorland of northern Europe and western Russia.

SIZE: HB 100–135 mm (3.9–5.3 in); TL 18–26 mm (0.7–1 in); WT 40–112 g (1.4–3.95 oz).

FORM: color a mixture of black and russet on back, with buffish-white on underparts and flanks; snout and face black, changing sharply to whitish in a line from the eyes and ears to the nose; pale russet stripes from crown to each eye. First digits have large, flattened claws for digging, which grow twice as long and wide in winter. Has very thick fur; even soles of feet are furred.

DIET: grasses, sedges and herbs, bark, roots, berries, lichens.

THE NORWAY LEMMING CAN BREED SO FAST THAT *sometimes its population outgrows its food supply. When this happens, large numbers of lemmings leave the area in a mass emigration in search of new supplies.*

BREEDING: 1–13 young born at a time, after a gestation of 16–23 days; several litters a year.

OTHER INFORMATION: lifespan up to 2 years. Burrows in tundra in summer, and under snow in winter. The snow insulates it from the cold above, so it has no need to hibernate. At the peak of a population cycle, there may be 250 lemmings per hectare (100 per acre).

CONSERVATION STATUS: not at risk.

EUROPEAN WATER VOLE

Arvicola amphibius

Water vole, Water rat
Family: Muridae

THE WATER VOLE IS AT HOME UNDER WATER. ITS *burrow in a river bank will probably have at least one underwater entrance. When threatened by danger on the bank, it dives into its burrow, then quietly slips out of another exit and swims away.*

DISTRIBUTION: ponds, lakes and streams of Europe, Russia and parts of southwestern Asia.

SIZE: HB 140–200 mm (5.6–8 in); TL 60–100 mm (2.4–4 in); WT 70–320 g (2.5–11.4 oz).

FORM: color light to dark brown, with buff or gray underparts. Tail and soles of hind feet hairy.

DIET: water plants, grasses, buds, fruits, roots, tubers, bulbs.

BREEDING: 1–11 young born at a time, after a gestation of 20–23 days.

OTHER INFORMATION: lifespan 2.5 years in the wild, over 3 in captivity. While some populations are aquatic, feeding mainly on water plants, others live far from water, making large burrow systems and leaving mounds of earth on the surface. Water vole burrows may be over 40 m (131 ft) long, with separate chambers for nests and winter food storage. The exits are linked above ground by runways

CONSERVATION STATUS: not at risk.

WOOD MOUSE

Apodemus sylvaticus

Common field mouse,
Long-tailed field mouse,
Eurasian wood mouse
Family: Muridae

THE WOOD MOUSE DOES NOT HIBERNATE IN WINTER,
*but it is not very active. It stores food in
underground larders to eat during the cold
weather. It will also raid human larders and
grain stores.*

DISTRIBUTION: fields, gardens, woodlands and forest edges from Iceland and western Europe south to northwest Africa and east to central and southwestern Asia and the Himalayas. May move into buildings in winter.

SIZE: HB 80–105 mm (3.2–4.2 in); TL 70–115 mm (2.8–4.6 in); WT 20–30 g (0.7–1.1 oz).

FORM: color dark yellowish-brown, underparts white with a sharp demarcation between upper and lower colors; there is a buff or yellowish-orange spot on the chest; tail dark brown above, whitish on underside.

DIET: mainly leaves, buds, seeds, fruits, berries; also nuts, bulbs, tubers, fungi, insects and spiders.

BREEDING: 2–9 young born at a time, in summer, after a gestation of 23 days; breeds several times a year.

OTHER INFORMATION: lifespan up to 4 years in captivity. Mainly nocturnal. If disturbed, it may hop away on its hind legs. Although it lives underground, it is a good climber and may forage for food high in the trees. It can also swim.

CONSERVATION STATUS: not at risk.

COMMON HAMSTER

Cricetus cricetus

Black-bellied hamster
Family: Muridae

DISTRIBUTION: dry grasslands, steppes, and cultivated land from Central Europe to Siberia.

SIZE: HB 200–270 mm (8–10.8 in); TL 50–70 mm (2–2.8 in); WT 220–460 g (0.7–16 oz).

FORM: color yellowish-brown to reddish-brown and white, with black underparts. Some animals may be albino or all black. Has large cheek pouches for carrying food.

DIET: leaves, seeds, fruits, roots, bulbs, invertebrates and small vertebrates.

BREEDING: 4–11 young born at a time, in spring and summer, after a gestation of 17–20 days; may breed twice a year.

THE COMMON HAMSTER'S LARGE CHEEK POUCHES ARE *used to carry food back to its burrow for storage. One hamster larder was found to contain some 90 kg (198 lb) of food. The hamster hibernates in winter, but wakes up from time to time to raid its larder.*

OTHER INFORMATION: lifespan about 2 years. Lives alone in a burrow with separate chambers for sleeping, storing food and defecating. Winter burrows are deeper than summer burrows, up to 2 m (6.6 ft) below the surface. When filled with air, its cheek pouches can be used to keep the hamster afloat while swimming.

CONSERVATION STATUS: not at risk, but in some areas numbers are decreasing where habitat is being cleared to make way for agriculture.

MONGOLIAN GERBIL

Meriones unguiculatus

Clawed jird
Family: Muridae

THE MONGOLIAN GERBIL LEAPS TO SAFETY ON ITS *large hind feet, heading for one of the entrances to its burrow. The burrows of large gerbil communities may have up to 18 entrances, providing plenty of potential escape routes.*

DISTRIBUTION: dry grasslands and steppes and semi-deserts of Mongolia and adjacent regions of Siberia and China.

SIZE: HB 100–125 mm (4–5 in); TL 95–110 mm (3.8–4.4 in); WT 70–130 g (2.5–4.6 oz).

FORM: color yellowish-brown to sandy- or grayish-yellow, with whitish under-parts and feet; may have light patches around face; tail has a dark tip. Tail about same length as body.

DIET: leaves and seeds.

BREEDING: 1–12 young born, after a gestation of 19–21 days; breeds up to 3 times a year. Males and earlier off-spring may help to bring up the young.

OTHER INFORMATION: lifespan over 2 years. Gets much of its water from early morning dew that gathers on seeds. Pet and laboratory gerbils are derived from this species. Does not hibernate in win-ter, but may spend long periods without emerging above ground, living on stored food. Alerts other gerbils to dan-ger by stamping its hind feet.

CONSERVATION STATUS: not at risk.

COMMON DORMOUSE

Muscardinus avellanarius

Hazel dormouse, Hazel mouse
Family: Muridae

*THE COMMON DORMOUSE IS
active mainly at night. Its
large whiskers help it find
its way in the dark;, it has
acute hearing, and uses a
range of sounds to make
contact with other dormice.*

DISTRIBUTION: forests, woodlands, hedgerows and thickets, from western Europe and southern Sweden to western Russia, eastern Europe and western Asia.

SIZE: HB 65–85 mm (2.6–3.4 in); TL 60–85 mm (2.4–3.4 in); WT 13–32 g (0.5–1.1 oz).

FORM: color tawny to orangey-brown, with yellowish-white underparts; throat and upper part of chest white.

DIET: leaves, buds, shoots, seeds, nuts, fruits, insects.

BREEDING: 1–7 young born at a time, after a gestation of 22–24 days; may breed twice a year.

OTHER INFORMATION: lifespan 4 years. Sleeps during day in a globular nest made of twigs, bark and grass. Hibernates in winter, under leaves on the woodland floor, in an old log or in a hollow tree stump.

CONSERVATION STATUS: not at risk, but numbers have fallen rapidly, as a result of the combined effects of past hunting, collecting for the pet trade and loss of its woodland habitat.

NORTH AMERICAN PORCUPINE

Erethizon dorsatum

Family: Erethizontidae

THE NORTH AMERICAN PORCUPINE *has over 30,000 sharp-tipped quills, which it erects when threatened. It whirls round to present its spiny rear and lashing, barbed tail to its attacker.*

DISTRIBUTION: throughout North America from northern Mexico northward, except for the extreme southwest, southeast and Gulf coast states.

SIZE: HB 645–930 mm (25.2–36.3 in); TL 125–300 mm (4.9–11.7 in); WT 3.5 –18 kg (7.7–40 lb). Quills up to 75 mm (2.9 in) long.

FORM: color black or brownish in east of range, yellowish in west, with dark underparts; quills have yellowish-white bases and dark tips.

DIET: leaves, buds, shoots, flowers, grasses, seeds, nuts, fruits, twigs.

BREEDING: only one young born at a time, rarely twins, in spring or early summer, after a gestation of 205–217 days; birth takes place in a tree cavity.

OTHER INFORMATION: lifespan up to 17 years in captivity. The quills are barbed; if they break off, they can work their way deep into their victim, sometimes puncturing vital organs.

CONSERVATION STATUS: not at risk.

AFRICAN PORCUPINE

Hystrix cristata

North African porcupine
Family: Hystricidae

THE AFRICAN PORCUPINE IS *a wary animal: if it meets another animal, or a human, it erects its spines, rattles its tail and stamps its feet. It may charge backward, attempting to drive its quills into the enemy.*

DISTRIBUTION: Italy, Sicily and the Mediterranean coast of North Africa south to northern Zaire and Tanzania, excluding much of the Sahara.

SIZE: HB 600–930 mm (23.4–36.3 in); TL 80–170 mm (3.1–6.6 in); WT 10–30 kg (22–66 lb).

FORM: color dark brown or black; quills have alternating light and dark bands; spines on mane, head and neck up to 400 mm (16 in) long, which can be erected to form a crest; tail has rattle-quills at tip; rear of back has very long quills, with some more flexible, whitish bristles projecting beyond.

DIET: roots, tubers, bulbs, fruits, bark, carrion.

BREEDING: 1–2 young born at a time, after a gestation of 93–105 days.

OTHER INFORMATION: lifespan about 15 years in the wild and over 20 in captivity. The hollow quills help give it buoyancy when swimming.

CONSERVATION STATUS: not at risk, but numbers are declining in the Mediterranean region as a result of persecution and by hunting for its meat.

CAPYBARA

Hydrochaeris hydrochaeris

Family: Hydrochaeridae

THE WORLD'S LARGEST RODENT, THE CAPYBARA IS *adapted for an aquatic life. Its eyes, ears and nostrils are on top of its head, so it can hide almost totally submerged for long periods. Its feet are partly webbed and it can swim underwater for some distance.*

DISTRIBUTION: rainforest or open country near rivers, lakes or swamps in Central and South America, from Panama east of the Andes to northeastern Argentina.

SIZE: HB 1–1.3 m (3.3–4.3 ft); tail absent; SH 400–500 mm (15.6–19.5 in); WT 37–66 kg (82–146 lb); female larger than male.

FORM: color light brown to reddish-brown or grayish-brown, with yellowish-brown underparts.

DIET: grasses and aquatic plants.

BREEDING: 1–7 young born at a time, after a gestation of 149–156 days.

OTHER INFORMATION: lifespan 10 years.

CONSERVATION STATUS: not at risk, but numbers are decreasing rapidly as a result of hunting for their meat and hides, and loss of habitat to pasture for livestock. They are now ranched in some areas.

GUINEA PIG

Cavia aperea

Wild cavy, Aperea
Family: Caviidae

THE GUINEA PIG WAS DOMESTI-
*cated in Peru about
6,000 years ago, and is
still reared for its meat in
many mountain villages.*

DISTRIBUTION: South America, from central Ecuador east to Suriname and south to southern Peru, Uruguay and northern Argentina, excluding the lower Amazon basin.

SIZE: HB 200–300 mm (8–12 in); no tail; WT 500–600 g (18–21 oz).

FORM: color grayish or brownish, with agouti-banded hairs; hair coarse and long; many color and hair variations in domestic varieties; 4 toes on forefeet, 3 on hind feet. Smaller, more slender and more agile than the domestic Guinea pig. Can leap to a height of 60 cm (2 ft).

DIET: grasses, leaves, flowers, fruits, seeds, roots, bark.

BREEDING: 1–5 young born, at a time, after about 62 days gestation. In large groups, only the most dominant females will breed. Young males are driven away when they reach sexual maturity at around 2–3 months.

OTHER INFORMATION: lifespan up to 8 years in captivity. Lives in groups of up to 20 individuals. Uses a wide range of sounds and scents to communicate.

CONSERVATION STATUS: not at risk.

CHINCHILLA

Chinchilla brevicaudata (C. laniger)

Family: Chinchillidae

DISTRIBUTION: the Andes of South America, from Peru to northern Chile.

SIZE: HB 225–380 mm (8.8–14.8 in); TL 75–150 mm (2.9–5.9 in); WT 500 –800 g (17.7–28.2 oz); female larger than male.

FORM: color brownish-gray or grayish-blue to pearl, with paler underparts. Fur dense, soft and silky. Forelegs short, hind legs long.

DIET: grasses, herbs, mosses, lichens.

BREEDING: 1–6 young born at a time, in summer, after 111–128 days gestation; may breed 2 or 3 times a year.

CHINCHILLAS HAVE THE LARGE EYES AND LONG *whiskers of nocturnal animals, but on sunny days they like to sunbathe. The thick, soft fur that protects them against the harsh mountain climate has, alas, led to their decline from overhunting.*

OTHER INFORMATION: lifespan up to 10 years in wild, over 20 in captivity. Nocturnal, sheltering by day in crevices among the rocks. Agile rock climbers, using their long hind legs for leaping. Live in large colonies that once numbered 100 individuals or more.

CONSERVATION STATUS: endangered by past and present hunting for their fur, and by burning and destruction of their mountain habitat.

NORTH AFRICAN GUNDI

Ctenodactylus gundi

Gundi
Family: Ctenodactylidae

DISTRIBUTION: rocky outcrops in deserts, semi-deserts and mountains of southeast Morocco, northwest Algeria, and Libya.

SIZE: HB about 200–240 mm (7.8–9.4 in); TL about 25–50 mm (0.98–1.5 in); WT about 190–360 g (6.7–12.7 oz).

FORM: color buff tinged with pale yellow or chestnut-brown, with paler underparts; tail short, pointing upward. Thick, silky fur insulates against heat by day and cold at night. Ears fringed with bristles to keep out sand. Feet have thick rubbery pads and sharp, hooked claws, which help it climb over steep rocks. Whiskers are long.

THE NORTH AFRICAN GUNDI USES A RANGE OF *chirping sounds to communicate across the desert. It emerges to feed at dawn, then sunbathes for a while before retreating to its hole to avoid the heat of the midday sun.*

DIET: grasses, herbs, leaves, stems, flowers, seeds.

BREEDING: 1–2 young born at a time, after a gestation of 69–79 days.

OTHER INFORMATION: lifespan up to 5 years in captivity. Active early morning and evening. Obtains all its water from its food. Does not store food, so spends a lot of time foraging. Lives in large, closely-related clans.

CONSERVATION STATUS: not at risk.

EUROPEAN RABBIT

Oryctolagus cuniculus

Rabbit, Old World rabbit
Family: Leporidae

THE EUROPEAN RABBIT HAS THRIVED WITH *the spread of agriculture, which has provided new food sources and new open ground in which to live. There are many domestic forms.*

DISTRIBUTION: southern France, the Iberian Peninsula and northwest Africa; introduced to rest of western Europe over 1,000 years ago; more recently to other parts of the world.

SIZE: HB 380–500 mm (14.8–19.5 in); TL 45–75 mm (1.8–2.9 in); WT 0.9–2 kg (2–4.4 lb).

FORM: color grayish, hairs often tipped with black or light brown; nape of neck yellowish-brown to reddish-brown; throat, belly and inner sides of legs pale gray to grayish-blue; underside of tail white. When alarmed, it stamps its foot, and runs for its burrow, flashing the white underside of its tail as a warning to other rabbits.

DIET: grasses, buds, shoots, roots, bark.

BREEDING: 1–9 young born at a time, after a gestation of 28–33 days; may breed up to 7 times a year.

OTHER INFORMATION: lifespan about 1.5 years in the wild, up to 10 in captivity. Lives in large communal burrows; each rabbit has its own chamber.

CONSERVATION STATUS: not at risk.

EUROPEAN HARE

Lepus europaeus

Brown hare, European brown hare,
Family: Leporidae

THE EUROPEAN HARE HAS LONG,
*powerful hind legs for bound-
ing across open country. It can
run at up to 80 km (50 mi)
per hour and cover 2.5 m
(8.2 ft) in a single leap.*

FORM: color brownish, with mixtures of black, gray or reddish-brown hairs; belly and underside of tail white.

DIET: grasses, herbs, buds, twigs, bark.

BREEDING: 1–5 young born at a time, in a simple depression in the grass, after a gestation of 42–43 days.

DISTRIBUTION: open country and forests of Europe and Russia, from Ireland (introduced) to western Siberia, and south through Central Asia to Iran. Introduced to North and South America.

SIZE: HB 500–760 mm (19.5–29.6 in); TL 70–120 mm (2.7–4.7 in); WT 2.5–6.5 kg (5.5–4.3 lb).

OTHER INFORMATION: lifespan up to 12 years. During the breeding season males rear up on their hind legs and "box" to win the rights to females. In winter in northern regions it may migrate up to 400 km (240 mi).

CONSERVATION STATUS: not at risk.

EASTERN COTTONTAIL

Sylvilagus floridanus

Florida cottontail
Family: Leporidae

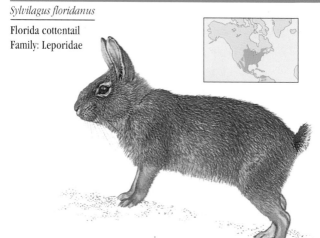

DISTRIBUTION: North and South America, from southern Manitoba and Quebec across the eastern and south-western United States to Costa Rica, Colombia and Venezuela.

SIZE: HB 375–483 mm (15–18.5 in); TL 39–65 mm (1.6–2.6 in); WT 0.9–1.5 kg (2–3.3 lb).

FORM: color brownish to grayish, with paler underparts; feet and underside of tail white.

DIET: grasses, herbs, vegetables, buds, shoots of shrubs and trees, twigs, bark.

BREEDING: 3–9 young born at a time, after a gestation of 25–35 days.

AN EASTERN COTTONTAIL ON THE *alert for danger. Rabbits have large mobile ears and good hearing. The position of their eyes at the sides of the head gives good all-round vision for detecting movements that might signal danger.*

OTHER INFORMATION: widely hunted for sport and for its meat, but its rapid breeding rate can compensate for this. Causes a lot of damage in young tree plantations by browsing on the new growth.

CONSERVATION STATUS: not at risk, but numbers are declining. Attempts have been made by hunting groups to reintroduce it to parts of the United States.

RUFOUS ELEPHANT-SHREW

Elephantulus rufescens

Family: Macroscelididae

THE RUFOUS ELEPHANT-SHREW IS A CAUTIOUS LITTLE *animal that feeds mainly on ants and termites. If alarmed, it rears up on its hind legs, tail held high, and bounds away at speed.*

DISTRIBUTION: grasslands, savannas and steppes of northeast Africa, from Sudan and Somalia to Tanzania.

SIZE: HB 125–140 mm (4.9–5.5 in); TL 130–140 mm (5.1–5.5 in); WT about 58 g (2.05 oz); female larger than male.

FORM: color sandy to brown, tinged with yellow; there is a white ring around the eyes and a black spot behind it.

DIET: insects and other invertebrates.

BREEDING: 1–2 young born at a time, after a gestation of 61–65 days.

OTHER INFORMATION: lifespan less than 2 years in the wild, up to 6 in captivity. Does not make its own burrows, but shelters in old logs, rock crevices or termite mounds; also in the abandoned burrows of other animals, provided they have at least two entrances. Lives in pairs and defends its territory.

CONSERVATION STATUS: not at risk.

COMMON TENREC

Tenrec ecaudatus

Tenrec, Tailless tenrec
Family: Tenrecidae

THE COMMON TENREC IS A PRIMITIVE HEDGEHOG-LIKE *animal from Madagascar. It produces larger litters (up to 32 young) and has more nipples than any other mammal. It has a relatively low body temperature, which may fall still further when inactive.*

DISTRIBUTION: most parts of Madagascar; introduced to the Comoros Islands and Reunion.

SIZE: HB 265–390 mm (10–16 in); TL 10–16 mm (0.4–0.62 in); WT 1.5–2.4 kg (3.3–5.3 lb).

FORM: grayish-brown, reddish-brown or yellowish-brown multicolored coat, sometimes with dark brown back and rump. Coat coarse and bristly, with rows of neck spines that form a crest, which is erected when alarmed.

DIET: invertebrates, small vertebrates, carrion and occasionally plants.

BREEDING: up to 32 young born at a time, in December and January, after a gestation of 56–64 days. A female tenrec has up to 29 nipples.

OTHER INFORMATION: lifespan over 6 years in captivity. Hibernates during the dry season in an underground burrow.

CONSERVATION STATUS: not immediately at risk, but numbers are declining.

GIANT OTTER SHREW

Potamogale velox

Giant African water shrew
Family: Tenrecidae

THE GIANT OTTER SHREW RESEMBLES A *miniature otter. It is a fast, agile swimmer, using sideways lashes of its powerful, flattened tail for propulsion. While underwater, its nostrils are closed with horny flaps.*

DISTRIBUTION: streams and pools in the rainforests of central Africa, at altitudes up to 1,800 m (5,908 ft), from Nigeria to western Kenya, northern Zambia and Angola.

SIZE: HB 290–350 mm (11.6–14 in); TL 245–290 mm (9.8–11.6 in); WT 340 –397 g (12–14 oz).

FORM: color chestnut-brown to dark brown or black with whitish or yellowish underparts. Digits of hind feet partly fused. Overall, the Giant otter shrew resembles an otter in appearance.

DIET: aquatic insects, crustaceans, larvae, fish, small amphibians. Hunts on land and in water.

BREEDING: 1–2 young born at a time, after an unknown gestation period.

OTHER INFORMATION: mainly nocturnal; hunts mainly by scent and touch. Shelters by day in burrows in stream banks, emerging through underwater exits. Lives alone in its own territory.

CONSERVATION STATUS: not at risk.

SOLENODON

Solenodon species

Family: Solenodontidae

DISTRIBUTION: forests and scrublands of Cuba, Haiti and the Dominican Republic.

SIZE: HB 280–330 mm (10.9–12.9 in); TL 220–250 mm (8.9–9.8 in); WT 0.7–1 kg (1.5–2.2 lb).

FORM: color of Hispaniola species (Haiti and Dominican Republic) brownish-gray, with yellowish flanks and black forehead; Cuban species dark gray, with paler head and underparts. In the Hispaniola species, the snout is joined to the skull by a ball-and-socket joint, which gives it more movement.

DIET: insects (especially millipedes and beetles), worms, termites, sometimes birds.

SOLENODONS ARE NOCTURNAL INSECT-EATERS THAT *root in the ground, under stones and logs, and in crevices with their long, flexible snouts. The snout is made of cartilage, not bone, and extends beyond the mouth.*

BREEDING: 1–2 young born at a time, after an unknown gestation period; may breed twice a year.

OTHER INFORMATION: nocturnal; emits high-pitched clicks, which are probably used for echolocation.

CONSERVATION STATUS: endangered.

159

EUROPEAN HEDGEHOG

Erinaceus europaeus

Western European hedgehog
Family: Erinaceidae

THE EUROPEAN HEDGEHOG *feeds mainly at night, hunting by smell. Its main defense is to roll into a ball, protecting its vulnerable underparts and erecting its spines.*

DISTRIBUTION: open woodlands, hedges, grasslands, parks and other urban areas of Europe, Russia and western Asia, excluding the far north; introduced to New Zealand.

SIZE: HB 250–300 mm (9.8–11.7 in); TL 20–30 mm (0.78–1.17 in); WT 0.4–1.1 kg (0.9–1.1 lb).

FORM: color varies from whitish to dark brown or black; spines have dark and light rings; underparts grayish to whitish.

DIET: insects, spiders, other invertebrates, small vertebrates, carrion, plants.

BREEDING: 2–10 young born, in spring and late summer, after a gestation of 31–37 days; often breeds twice a year.

OTHER INFORMATION: lifespan 8 years. Hibernates in winter in colder regions. Lives in a specific "home range", centered on a shelter, such as a rock crevice, pile of wood or burrow. Has a strange habit of "self-anointing": producing foamy spit and flicking it over its spines with its tongue.

CONSERVATION STATUS: not at risk.

DESERT HEDGEHOG

Paraechinus aethiopicus

Ethiopean hedgehog
Family: Erinaceidae

THE DESERT HEDGEHOG HAS LARGE EARS AND ACUTE *hearing, an adaptation to its nocturnal lifestyle. Unlike the European hedgehog, it may dig its own burrows for shelter from the desert heat.*

DISTRIBUTION: deserts and semi-deserts of Northern Africa and the Middle East, from Mauritania and Morocco to northern Somalia, Arabia and Iraq.

SIZE: HB 140–230 mm (5.5–9 in); TL 10–40 mm (0.4–1.6 in); WT 400 –700 g (14.1–25 oz).

FORM: color dark on back, with light-tipped spines that may be mainly dark brown, black, white or yellow; forehead, cheeks and belly whitish; snout and face chocolate brown to almost black.

DIET: insects, scorpions and other invertebrates, small vertebrates, eggs.

BREEDING: 1–5 young born at a time, between July and September, after a gestation of about 35–39 days.

OTHER INFORMATION: lifespan over 4 years in captivity.

CONSERVATION STATUS: not at risk but the Egyptian subspecies *Paraechinus aethiopicus wassifi* may be extinct.

161

COMMON SHREW

Sorex araneus

European common shrew, Eurasian common shrew
Family: Soricidae

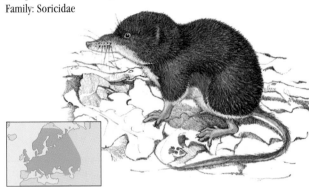

THE COMMON SHREW IS CONSTANTLY ON THE GO: *it needs to hunt day and night all year round to get enough food. A small animal, it has a large surface area to volume ratio, so it loses heat easily, and must rely on a regular supply of food to produce more.*

DISTRIBUTION: in most habitats, from western Europe to western Russia.

SIZE: HB 55–82 mm (2.1–3.2 in); TL 31–52 mm (1.2–2 in); WT 6–10 g (0.21–0.35 oz).

FORM: color brown on back and tail, sometimes black or reddish, with nut-brown flanks and grayish underparts and underside of tail. Glands in the skin secrete substances that are distasteful to potential predators.

DIET: worms, insects and other invertebrates, carrion.

BREEDING: 2–10 young born at a time after a gestation of 19–21 days; often breeds twice a year.

OTHER INFORMATION: lifespan 12–16 months. Solitary and aggressive. Defends a territory ranging in size from 100 to over 3,000 sq m (120–3,588 sq yd). Territories are marked with scent. The pitch and intensity of its high-pitched calls are thought to convey dominance information and help avoid fights. Also produces ultrasound, which may be used for echolocation.

CONSERVATION STATUS: not at risk.

162

EUROPEAN MOLE

Talpa europaea

Common mole
Family: Talpidae

DISTRIBUTION: grasslands, fields, gardens and forest clearings from Europe (except Ireland) east to the rivers Ob and Irtysh in Russia and south to the Mediterranean.

SIZE: HB 110–170 mm (4.3–6.6 in); TL 20–34 mm (0.8–1.3 in); WT 60–120 g (2.1–4.2 oz).

FORM: color usually black, sometimes with a silvery sheen, with paler underparts; some individuals may be cinnamon, cream or golden. The soft, velvety fur is easily brushed forward or back, so offers little resistance to its movement in either direction in the tunnel. Eyes are minute.

THE EUROPEAN MOLE SPENDS MOST OF ITS LIFE *underground, out of sight of predators. It excavates tunnels through the soil with the powerful claws on its front paws, and feeds on worms and insects it finds there.*

DIET: worms and insects; also small vertebrates such as lizards, snakes, small birds and mice.

BREEDING: 2–9 young born, in spring, after a gestation of 35–42 days.

OTHER INFORMATION: lifespan up to 4 years. Mounds of earth thrown up on the surface betray the presence of mole tunnels below.

CONSERVATION STATUS: not at risk.

STAR-NOSED MOLE

Condylura cristata
Family: Talpidae

DISTRIBUTION: near lakes, rivers and streams in eastern North America, from Manitoba and Labrador south to Georgia and North Carolina.

THE STAR-NOSED MOLE HAS 22 FLESHY PINK *tentacles on the end of its snout. These are in constant motion while it swims, perhaps helping it sense the vibrations or scent of its prey.*

SIZE: HB 100–127 mm (3.9–5 in); TL 76–89 mm (3–3.5 in); WT 40–80 g (1.4–2.8 oz).

FORM: color brownish-black to black, with pink, hairless fleshy star-like processes on snout. These become fatter in both sexes in winter; they are thought to contain fat reserves for the breeding season. The fur is dense and water-repellent.

DIET: aquatic insects, crustaceans, earthworms and other invertebrates, small fish. It mainly forages underground; also on the surface at night and also hunts under water.

BREEDING: 2–7 young born, from April to June; unknown gestation period.

OTHER INFORMATION: unlike other moles, male and female stay together after mating. Also sometimes lives in colonies, sharing a network of underground tunnels that may go as deep as 60 cm (2 ft). Will hunt under the ice in ponds in winter.

CONSERVATION STATUS: not at risk.

PYRENEAN DESMAN

Galemys pyrenaicus

Family: Talpidae

THE PYRENEAN DESMAN HUNTS MAINLY AT NIGHT. IT *has poor vision, but the long sensitive snout has an excellent sense of touch; the desman also uses echolocation.*

DISTRIBUTION: by swift-flowing streams in the French and Spanish Pyrenees, and the mountains of northern Spain and northern Portugal, at altitudes up to about 2,200 m (7,000 ft).

SIZE: HB 97–133 mm (3.8–5.2 in); TL 130–155 mm (5.1–6 in); WT 35–80 g (1.2–2.8 oz); snout about 20 mm (0.78 in) long.

FORM: color dark grayish-brown to dark brown with metallic luster; underparts pale gray; snout and feet dark; tail whitish. Feet are webbed and fringed with stiff bristles for swimming. The hind feet are the main source of propulsion when swimming. Tail rounded.

DIET: aquatic invertebrates such as insects, crustaceans and worms, and small fish.

BREEDING: 1–5 young born at a time, after a gestation of about 30 days.

OTHER INFORMATION: lifespan 4 years. Lives in pairs. It is aggressive and will fight intruders that invade its territory, which is marked by scent. Shelters by day in holes in the river bank. Uses long snout as a snorkel under water.

CONSERVATION STATUS: at risk mainly by pollution of its mountain streams.

Myrmecophaga tridactyla

Family: Myrmecophagidae

THE GIANT ANTEATER HAS A GIANT-SIZED APPETITE: *it can consume up to 35,000 termites a day. To protect the large curved claws on its front feet, used for tearing into termite nests, it walks on its knuckles.*

DISTRIBUTION: grasslands, swamps, and rainforests of Central and South America, from Belize to northern Argentina.

SIZE: HB 1.0–1.3 m (3.3–4.3 ft); TL 650–900 mm (25–35 in); WT 30–35 kg (66–77 lb).

FORM: color grayish-brown with dark, white-fringed, broad diagonal stripe from shoulders to mid-back; front legs whitish on outer surface, with a dark ring just above the paws. It has a 55cm (21 in) long tongue that can be flicked in and out 160 times a minute for picking up its prey.

DIET: ants, termites, insect larvae; sometimes fruit.

BREEDING: only one young born at a time, in spring, after a gestation of 180–190 days. Mother carries young on her back for up to one year.

OTHER INFORMATION: lifespan over 25 years in captivity. A shy, solitary animal, its sharp claws provide a formidable defense as it rears up on its hind legs to lash at its enemy.

CONSERVATION STATUS: not immediately at risk, but populations shrinking.

THREE-TOED SLOTH

Bradypus variegatus

Brown-throated three-toed sloth
Family: Bradypodidae

THE BROWN-THROATED
three-toed sloth spends
most of its life hanging upside
down, feeding on leaves. Blue-green
algae living in its coat color it greenish,
enhancing its camouflage.

DISTRIBUTION: rainforests of Central and South America, from Honduras to northern Argentina.

SIZE: HB 500–700 mm (19.5–27.3 in); TL 38–90 mm (1.5–3.5 in); WT 2.25–5.5 kg (5–12 lb).

FORM: color grayish-brown; shoulders and upper back have striking orange patch with black border and black stripe down the middle; face and forehead white with dark stripes over eyes; top of head almost black; throat brown. Hairs all point toward center of back, the opposite of other mammals.

DIET: leaves and buds of many different tree species. Its slow, lazy lifestyle requires little energy, so it can survive on leaves of low nutrient status, and is not in competition with other herbivores. They also maintain a low body temperature, which saves energy.

BREEDING: only one young born at a time, after a gestation of 120–180 days.

OTHER INFORMATION: lifespan probably 30–40 years. It usually visits the ground only to defecate.

CONSERVATION STATUS: not at risk, but numbers are declining as a result of deforestation.

NINE-BANDED ARMADILLO

Dasypus novemcinctus

Common long-nosed armadillo
Great banded armadillo
Family: Dasypodidae

THE NINE-BANDED ARMADILLO FEEDS MAINLY *on ants, termites and grubs, which it catches with its long tongue coated in sticky saliva. The tough skin on its snout protects it from the bites.*

DISTRIBUTION: grasslands, swamps, cultivated land and rainforests up to 3,000 m (9,846 ft) in North and South America, from the southern United States to northern Argentina, excluding South America west of the Andes.

SIZE: HB 355–570 mm (13.8–22 in); TL 25–45 mm (0.98–1.75 in); WT 2.65 –6.25 kg (5.8–13.8 lb).

FORM: color pinkish-brown, paler on flanks and underparts, with 8–11 distinct bands of "armor".

DIET: insects, termites, beetles and their larvae, grubs, worms, snails and other invertebrates, small vertebrates, carrion; shoots, fruits, mushrooms, bulbs, tubers.

BREEDING: usually produce quadruplets of the same sex (derived from the same fertilized egg), in February or March, after 120 days gestation.

OTHER INFORMATION: lifespan up to 15 years in the wild, 19 in captivity. The armor develops at an early age. If threatened, an armadillo will dash to the nearest burrow, but if this is too far away, it will roll into a ball, so that its armor protects its often vulnerable underparts.

CONSERVATION STATUS: not at risk.

SMALL-SCALED TREE PANGOLIN

Manis tricuspis

Three-pointed pangolin,
African tree pangolin
Family: Manidae

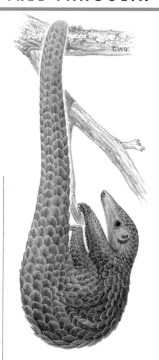

A SMALL-SCALED TREE PANGOLIN HANGS BY ITS TAIL *from a branch. The tail has a bare patch at the tip to assist its grip. Tiny pebbles in the pangolin's stomach help to break down the hard outer casings of its ant and termite prey.*

DISTRIBUTION: forest floor and lower branches of African rainforests, from Senegal to western Kenya, and south to Zambia.

SIZE: HB 340–450 mm (13.3–17.6 in); TL 400–500 mm (15.6–19.5 in); WT 1.8–2.4 kg (4–5.3 lb); male larger than female.

FORM: color brownish-gray scales over whitish skin and hair. Scales on back have 3 points. Tail is prehensile; also used as a support when climbing trees.

DIET: ants and termites. Tough skin on the snout protects against insect bites and stings, and the ear openings and nostrils can be closed.

BREEDING: only one young born at a time, after a gestation of about 150 days. The young rides on the back of its mother's tail.

OTHER INFORMATION: when threatened, a pangolin can roll up so it is completely encased in armor.

CONSERVATION STATUS: not at risk.

SMOKY BAT

Furipterus horrens

Thumbless bat
Family: Furipteridae

DISTRIBUTION: Central and South America, from Costa Rica to Peru and Brazil; also on Trinidad.

SIZE: HB 30–40 mm (1.2–1.6 in); TL 24–36 mm (0.9–1.4 in); forearm length 30–40 mm (1.2–1.6 in); WT about 3 g (0.1 oz).

FORM: color ranges from slaty-blue to dark gray or brownish-gray, with paler underparts. Has much reduced thumb, which is enclosed within wing membrane so that only the small claw protrudes. Wings and legs relatively long. Ears widely separated, funnel-shaped with broad bases that cover the eyes. Snout pig-like, slightly upturned.

SMOKY BATS ARE SOMETIMES CALLED THUMBLESS BATS, *because their tiny thumbs are almost entirely enclosed within the flight membrane. They are slow-flying bats that hunt not far above the forest floor.*

DIET: insects, especially moths. Forages by flying 1–5 m (3.3–16.4 ft) above the forest floor.

BREEDING: details not known.

OTHER INFORMATION: roosts in caves or hollow trees, in mixed-sex colonies of up to 250 individuals, usually divided into a number of separate roosting clusters.

CONSERVATION STATUS: not known.

170

KITTI'S HOG-NOSED BAT

Craseonycteris thonglongyai

Butterfly bat, Bumblebee bat
Family: Craseonycteridae

KITTI'S HOG-NOSED BAT IS THE *smallest bat, and probably the smallest mammal, in the world. About the size of a bumblebee, it has long, wide wings capable of hovering flight.*

DISTRIBUTION: limestone caves by the River Kwai, in western Thailand.

SIZE: HB 29–33 mm (1.1–1.3 in); no tail; forearm length 22–26 mm (0.9–1 in); WT about 2 g (0.07 oz).

FORM: two color phases are known, with grayish or reddish upper parts; underparts paler; wings and wing membranes darker. Ears large; eyes small, almost hidden in fur; thumb short, with well-developed claw; hind feet long and slender.

DIET: very small insects and spiders; takes prey from foliage as well as in the air. Forages around teak trees and bamboo clumps.

BREEDING: details not known.

OTHER INFORMATION: roosts in small groups of 10–15 individuals deep inside caves.

CONSERVATION STATUS: endangered; total population only about 200 animals, from a single location, so extremely vulnerable to habitat disturbance. This unique animal first became known to science in the early 1970s.

GREATER HORSESHOE BAT

Rhinolophus ferrumequinum

Family: Rhinolophidae

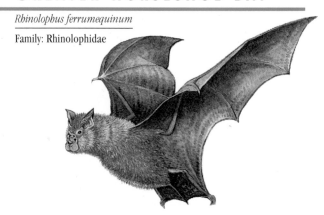

LIKE MOST INSECT-EATING BATS, THE GREATER *horseshoe bat hunts by echolocation: it emits pulses of ultrasound (high-pitched sound) and analyzes the echoes reflected from objects. The noseleaf helps to focus these sounds.*

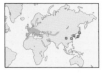

DISTRIBUTION: temperate and subtropical regions of the Old World, from southern England and Wales to central and southern Europe and Morocco, and east to Afghanistan and Japan.

SIZE: HB about 70 mm (2.7 in); TL about 32 mm (1.25 in); forearm length about 51 mm (2 in); WT 27.3 –23.4 g (0.96–0.83 oz).

FORM: color ashy-gray above, with pale buff underparts, sometimes tinged with pink or yellow. Noseleaf horseshoe-shaped. Ears large and wide, with sharp recurved tip.

DIET: insects. Leaves roost early in the evening and flies at intervals during the night. Hunts low over the ground.

BREEDING: one young born at a time, rarely two, after 60–75 days gestation.

OTHER INFORMATION: lifespan over 18 years.

CONSERVATION STATUS: numbers are declining as a result of disturbance of its roosts in buildings and caves, and changes to the habitat that have reduced the numbers of large insects.

NOCTULE BAT

Nyctalus noctula

Family: Vespertilionidae

A NOCTULE BAT HOMES IN ON ITS INSECT PREY, *pinpointing its location by the use of ultrasound pulses. It is an agile flyer, capable of making quick turns.*

DISTRIBUTION: forests and countryside near human settlements from southern Scandinavia, Scotland and Ireland south to Morocco; east across temperate Asia to Japan, Burma and Taiwan.

SIZE: HB 69–82 mm (2.7–3.2 in); TL 41–59 mm (1.6–2.3 in); forearm length 45–55 mm (1.75–2.1 in); WT 15–40 g (0.53–1.41 oz).

FORM: color reddish-brown. A large bat with an arched snout, short round ears and long narrow wings.

DIET: large insects. Flies just before sunset, and again before dawn.

BREEDING: 1–2, rarely 3, young born at a time, after a gestation of about 50–70 days.

OTHER INFORMATION: lifespan 8 years. Roosts mainly in tree hollows. Hibernates in winter often in buildings. Reported to migrate over distances as long as 2,347 km (1,458 mi).

CONSERVATION STATUS: numbers are declining as a result of loss of its woodland habitat, especially of large roosting trees, and loss of insect prey due to changing farming practices.

173

LARGE MOUSE-EARED BAT

Myotis myotis

Greater mouse-eared bat
Family: Vespertilionidae

A LARGE MOUSE-EARED BAT IN FLIGHT.
*A bat's wing membranes are supported
by the forearms and the greatly elongated
fingers. The thumbs are reduced to short
hooked structures that are useful when
clambering in trees or caves.*

DISTRIBUTION: open woodlands, forest
edges and pastures of central and
southern Europe and the Middle East.

SIZE: HB 68–82 mm (2.7–3.2 in);
TL 48–60 mm (1.9–2.3 in); forearm
length 59–68 mm (2.3–2.7 in); WT 19
–45 g (0.67–1.59 oz).

FORM: color brownish, with paler
underparts. Tip of tail extends freely
beyond flight membrane. Hangs freely
from roof of roosts.

DIET: insects, especially moths and
beetles. Flies only after dark. Takes
insects in the air and on the ground.

BREEDING: one young born, rarely
twins, in late spring or early summer,
after a gestation of up to 70 days.

OTHER INFORMATION: lifespan 18
years. Hibernates in winter. Migrates
between summer and winter roosts.

CONSERVATION STATUS: numbers are
declining rapidly in most parts of its
range; it is almost extinct in Britain,
the Low Countries and Israel.

SPECTRAL VAMPIRE

Vampyrum spectrum

Linnaeus's false vampire bat
Family: Phyllostomidae

THE SPECTRAL VAMPIRE IS THE *largest bat in the New World. It was once thought to drink blood, but is actually a carnivore.*

DIET: small vertebrates such as birds, other bats, rats and mice; also insects and fruits. Hunts at twilight by patient stalking of its prey.

DISTRIBUTION: lowland forests, swamps and gardens of Central and South America, from southern Mexico to Peru and central Brazil, and on Trinidad.

SIZE: HB 125–135 mm (4.9–5.3 in); tail absent; forearm length 100–108 mm (3.9–4.2 in); WT 145–190 g (5.1–6.7 oz).

FORM: reddish-brown, with paler underparts. Ears very large and noseleaf pronounced.

BREEDING: only one young born at a time, after an unknown gestation period. Male helps care for mother and young, wrapping his wings around them in their roosts.

OTHER INFORMATION: kills prey by a bite to the skull. Roosts in hollow trees and buildings.

CONSERVATION STATUS: not known.

YELLOW-WINGED BAT

Lavia frons

African yellow-
winged bat
Family: Megadermatidae

THE YELLOW-WINGED BAT
hunts like a fly-catcher,
hanging from a favorite perch until
an insect comes within reach, then
darting down, seizing its prey and
bringing it back to the perch to eat.

DISTRIBUTION: forests and open country of Africa, Gambia to Ethiopia, and
south to Zambia.

SIZE: HB 58–80 mm (2.3–3.1 in);
no external tail; forearm length 49–
63 mm (1.9–2.5 in); WT 28–36 g
(0.99–1.27 oz).

FORM: color bluish-gray to olive-green,
with yellowish-orange wings and ears.
Underparts occasionally yellowish.
Ears very large, joined over forehead.
Noseleaf prominent .

DIET: insects, spiders and small vertebrates. Hunts especially around flower-
ing acacia trees; also among grasses.

BREEDING: one young born at a time,
rarely twins, at start of rainy season in
April, after a gestation of 3–5 months.

OTHER INFORMATION: often seen during the day. Lives in permanent territorial pairs, defending a feeding territory
of up to 0.95 ha (2.35 acres). Roosts in
trees up to (10 m) 33 ft above ground;
also in hollow trees and buildings.

CONSERVATION STATUS: not at risk, but
locally affected by land use changes.

MEXICAN LONG-NOSED BAT

Leptonycteris nivalis

Family: Phyllostomidae

THE MEXICAN LONG-NOSED BAT FEEDS *on nectar and pollen. Its long snout can probe the flowers of cacti and agaves, and it also has a tongue 76mm (2.85 in) long covered in bristles that help to pick up the nectar.*

DISTRIBUTION: high pine and oak woodlands of North and Central America, from southern Texas to Guatemala.

SIZE: HB 70–95 mm (2.7–3.7 in); tail minute; forearm 46–57 mm (1.8–2.2 in); WT 18–30 g (0.64–1.06 oz).

FORM: color reddish-brown to blackish-brown, with cinnamon or brown underparts. Snout long.

DIET: nectar, pollen, fruits; probably also any insects found on them. Has sharp canine teeth that can break into cactus fruits.

BREEDING: probably only one young born at a time; unknown gestation.

OTHER INFORMATION: roosts in large colonies, sometimes containing over 10,000 bats. Very important pollinator of cacti flowers.

CONSERVATION STATUS: endangered by loss of habitat, especially by clearing of agaves, and by human persecution.

177

LONG-NOSED ECHIDNA

Zaglossus bruijni

Long-nosed spiny anteater
Family: Tachyglossidae

THE LONG-NOSED ECHIDNA IS *a monotreme, or egg-laying mammal. The female develops a temporary pouch during the breeding season, where the egg is incubated. Mammary glands open into this pouch, providing milk.*

DISTRIBUTION: New Guinea and nearby Salawatti Island, in mountain forests and alpine meadows up to 4,000 m (13,128 ft).

SIZE: HB 450–770 mm (17.6–30 in); tail negligible; WT 5–10 kg (11–22 lb).

FORM: color of fur black or brownish; spines vary from black to gray or white. Head usually paler than body. Spines much shorter than in Short-nosed echidna; limbs quite long, with stout claws on middle three toes of each foot. Male has a spur on inner surface of each hind leg, near foot. Snout long.

DIET: earthworms. Picks up its food with its long tongue; a furrow on the upper side of the tongue contains 3 rows of horny backward-pointing teeth, on which the prey is impaled.

BREEDING: details not known.

OTHER INFORMATION: lifespan up to 31 years in captivity. A solitary, nocturnal animal. When threatened, it can dig rapidly into the ground, so that only the spiny part of its body is left facing the enemy. Alternatively, an echidna may wedge itself into a crevice. If the ground is too hard to dig, it rolls up into a ball, so its spines stick out all round, like a hedgehog.

CONSERVATION STATUS: threatened by loss of its forest habitat to agriculture and by hunting for its meat.

PLATYPUS

Ornithorhynchus anatinus

Duck-billed platypus
Family: Ornithorhynchidae

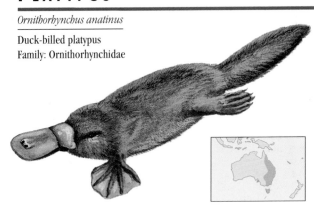

DISTRIBUTION: lakes, rivers and streams of eastern Australia, from Queensland to Tasmania; introduced to Kangaroo Island, South Australia.

SIZE: HB 300–450 mm (11.7–17.6 in); TL 100–150 mm (3.9–5.9 in); WT 0.5 –2 kg (1.1–4.4 lb); male largest.

FORM: color dark brown; underparts silvery-gray to light brown, with a rusty-brown midline. Feet webbed for swimming.

DIET: aquatic invertebrates such as snails, shrimps, insects and their larvae. It is thought to use electrical stimuli to find its prey.

BREEDING: the platypus is a mono-treme, or egg-laying mammal. 1–3

THE DUCK-BILLED PLATYPUS SWIMS BY ROWING *alternately first with one foreleg, then with the other, using its flattened tail as a rudder. It probes the river bed for invertebrates with its highly sensitive, duck-like bill.*

eggs are laid at a time, about 2 weeks after mating. It incubates the eggs by curling around them in a nest of leaves in a burrow in the river bank until they hatch, usually 7–10 days later.

OTHER INFORMATION: lifespan up to 17 years in captivity. The eyes and ears lie in furrows that can be closed while under water, as can the nostrils.

CONSERVATION STATUS: not at risk; numbers were seriously reduced earlier this century by hunting for its pelt, but conservation efforts have enabled popu-lations to recover.

VIRGINIA OPOSSUM

Didelphis virginianus

Common opossum, Northern opossum
Family: Didelphidae

THE VIRGINIA OPOSSUM MAY GIVE BIRTH TO UP TO
*56 young, but has only 13 teats, so most
will die. The survivors are all carried in
their mother's pouch or, when they become
too big for it, on her back.*

DISTRIBUTION: moist forest and scrub
of North and Central America, from
New Hampshire and southern Ontario
to Costa Rica; still expanding its range
northward – the northernmost of all
the marsupials.

SIZE: HB 325–500 mm (12.7–19.5 in);
TL 255–535 mm (9.95–20.9 in);
WT 2–5.5 kg (4.4–12.1 lb).

FORM: color varies from white and
cream to brown and black; ears black;
may have dark streaks on head.

DIET: earthworms and other invertebrates, mice, rats, birds, frogs, carrion,
fruit and other plant material.

BREEDING: up to 21 young born at a
time, after about 12–15 days gestation.

OTHER INFORMATION: lifespan up to 3
years in the wild, 8 in captivity. When
threatened, the opossum may "play
possum", feigning death.

CONSERVATION STATUS: not at risk.

WHITE-EARED OPOSSUM

Didelphis albiventris

Southern opossum
Family: Didelphidae

OPOSSUMS ARE EXPERT TREE *climbers. The powerful prehensile tail is naked for much of its length, which gives it a strong enough grip to support the animal's entire weight. It is also used for collecting nesting material.*

DISTRIBUTION: forests of South America, from Colombia and Venezuela to Paraguay.

SIZE: HB about 325 mm (12.7 in); TL about 255 mm (9.95 in); WT about 2 kg (4.4 lb).

FORM: color grayish, reddish or black; may have three dark streaks on head, the lateral ones running through the eyes; most of tail naked; ears pink.

DIET: earthworms, insects, frogs, birds, mice, rats, carrion, fruits.

BREEDING: 2–7 young born at a time, after a gestation of 12–13 days; may have more than one litter a year.

OTHER INFORMATION: moves rapidly on the ground, but prefers to be in trees. The large toe on each foot is opposable for improved grip. A solitary, nocturnal animal, it is aggressive if it meets a neighbor. Has acute hearing, plus excellent senses of smell and touch.

CONSERVATION STATUS: not at risk, but is persecuted in some areas for its raids on poultry and eggs.

LITTLE WATER OPOSSUM

Lutreolina crassicaudata

Lutrine opossum, Thick-tailed opossum
Family: Didelphidae

DISTRIBUTION: grasslands and riverine woodlands of South America east of the Andes from Bolivia and southern Brazil to Paraguay, Uruguay and northern Argentina.

SIZE: HB 250–400 mm (9.8–15.6 in); TL 210–310 mm (8.2–12.1 in); WT 200–540 g (7.1–19.1 oz).

FORM: color varies from yellowish-brown or buff to golden red or dark brown, with reddish, yellowish, buff or dark brown underparts. Has a low, streamlined body with short, stout legs, small ears and a thick tail that is densely furred, particularly at the base. It is an excellent climber.

THE LITTLE WATER OPOSSUM HAS A THICK TAIL, WHICH *is used to store fat. Its streamlined body is well suited to swimming and diving, but its fur is not water repellent.*

DIET: worms, insects and other invertebrates; small vertebrates, including fish; fruits, seeds. It is an able predator in water, trees and on the ground.

BREEDING: about 4 young born at a time, after a gestation of about 10 days; breeds twice a year.

OTHER INFORMATION: builds nests in reeds at edges of ponds and streams. Does not develop a pouch.

CONSERVATION STATUS: not at risk.

YAPOK

Chironectes minimus

Water opossum
Family: Didelphidae

THE YAPOK IS THE ONLY FULLY AQUATIC MARSUPIAL.
*It has a streamlined body with dense fur
that repels water and webbed hind feet; the
female's pouch opens backward and can be
closed by a strong muscle.*

DISTRIBUTION: ponds, lakes and
streams of Central and South America,
up to almost 2,000 m (6,564 ft),
from Central America to southern
Brazil; possibly also on Trinidad.

SIZE: HB 260–400 mm (10.1–15.6 in);
TL 310–430 mm (12.1–16.8 in);
WT 604–790 g (21.3–27.9 oz).

FORM: color blocks of black fur separated by gray, except for a black band
along midline of back; underparts and
chin gray or whitish; snout and head
blackish, with grayish-white band.

DIET: aquatic insects and crustaceans,
fish, small riverbank mammals.

BREEDING: 2–5 young born; develop
faster than other marsupials, spending
only about 14 days in the pouch.

OTHER INFORMATION: lifespan almost
3 years in captivity. Both sexes have a
pouch. The male uses his to protect his
sexual organs while swimming.

CONSERVATION STATUS: probably not
at risk, but rare throughout its range.

KULTARR

Antechinomys laniger

Family: Dasyuridae

THE KULTARR IS A NOCTURNAL MARSUPIAL MOUSE. *It is a very fast runner, with large feet and cushion-like soles. Long touch-sensitive hairs grow from its snout and wrists.*

DISTRIBUTION: scattered populations in savannas, dry grasslands and deserts of inland Australia, from Western Australia to New South Wales and Queensland. Its range has been fragmented by clearing of land for agriculture and burning of grassland.

SIZE: HB 80–110 mm (3.2–4.3 in); TL 100–145 mm (3.9–5.7 in); WT 20–35 g (0.7–1.2 oz); male larger than female.

FORM: color buffish-gray, with white underparts; darker ring around eye;

dark patch in middle of forehead; lower part of tail buff, tip brown or black, with long hairs. Body fur long and soft.

DIET: invertebrates, especially insects, spiders and centipedes.

BREEDING: up to 6 young born at a time, after a gestation of 12 days.

OTHER INFORMATION: lifespan almost 3 years in captivity. Solitary; nests in hollow logs and tree stumps, in the burrows of other animals or in dense vegetation.

CONSERVATION STATUS: endangered in New South Wales and Queensland; scattered distribution elsewhere.

SPOTTED-TAIL QUOLL

Dasyurus maculatus

Tiger cat
Family: Dasyuridae

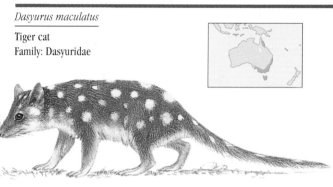

DISTRIBUTION: dense, moist forests of eastern Australia and Tasmania; now rare on the mainland.

SIZE: HB 350–759 mm (13.7–29.6 in); TL 340–550 mm (13.3–21.5 in); WT 4–7 kg (8.8–15.4 lb); male larger than female.

FORM: reddish-brown to dark brown, with white flecks that extend down tail; underparts paler.

DIET: mammals up to the size of wallabies and small kangaroos; birds; sometimes insects and plant material.

BREEDING: 4–6 young born at a time, in winter, after a gestation of 21 days.

OTHER INFORMATION: lifespan up to 4 years in captivity. Has a lengthy, rather

THE SPOTTED-TAIL QUOLL HUNTS BOTH ON THE *ground and in the trees. It is a good climber, and can catch birds while they are asleep in the trees at night. It attacks its prey with a sweep of the forepaws, killing with a bite to the neck, just like true cats.*

rough courtship, in which the female is often seized by the head and neck, inflicting injuries. Both parents look after the young, which leave the pouch at 7 weeks and are fully independent at 18 weeks.

CONSERVATION STATUS: threatened by destruction of its forest habitat, and by widespread trapping and poisoning for its alleged raids on poultry; also by introduced predators such as domestic cats, domestic dogs and foxes. Rare in Tasmania as a result of a disease that wiped out many quolls early in the twentieth century.

FAT-TAILED DUNNART

Sminthopsis crassicaudata

Thick-tailed dunnart
Family: Dasyuridae

THE FAT-TAILED DUNNART LIVES IN DRY *areas; fat is built up in its tail to provide it with nutrients when insects are scarce. The blood vessels in the large ears help to keep it cool by radiating heat.*

DISTRIBUTION: drier parts of inland southern Australia.

SIZE: HB 70–120 mm (2.7–4.7 in); TL 55–130 mm (2.1–5.1 in); WT 10–15 g (0.35–0.53 oz).

FORM: color buffish-gray, with white or grayish-white underparts; feet white; tail grayish or brown. Feet narrow. Tail becomes very fat when food is plentiful. Eyes and ears large.

DIET: mainly insects and spiders plus their larvae; also small vertebrates such as mice and lizards. Hunts at night.

BREEDING: 3–10 young born at a time, after a gestation of about 13 days; usually breeds twice a year. When food is scarce, it may enter a deep sleep, allowing its body to cool down and thus saving energy. While asleep, it lives off the fat stored in its tail. Nests in hollows between stones or in hollow logs. Solitary during the breeding season, but nests in groups of 2–8 at other times.

OTHER INFORMATION: lifespan about 18 months in the wild; up to 4 years in captivity.

CONSERVATION STATUS: not at risk.

TASMANIAN WOLF

Thylacinus cynocephalus

Thylacine, Tasmanian tiger
Family: Thylacinidae

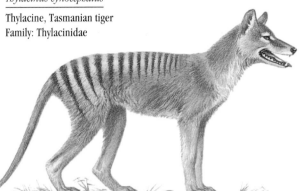

THE TASMANIAN WOLF RESEMBLED A WOLF, BUT WAS A
*true marsupial, using a pouch for breeding.
It hunted at night, pursuing its prey until it
became exhausted and could be overpowered.*

DISTRIBUTION: probably extinct.
Formerly inhabited forests and grasslands of southwestern Tasmania.

SIZE: HB 1–1.3 m (3.3–4.3 ft); TL 500
–650 mm (19.5–25.4 in); SH about
600 mm (23.4 in); WT 15–35 kg
(33–77 lb).

FORM: tawny-gray or sandy-yellow,
with black or brown stripes across back;
underparts paler; white markings
around eyes and ears. Dog-like form.

DIET: mainly mammals, such as kangaroos, wallabies and bandicoots.

BREEDING: 2–4 young born at a time,
after an unknown gestation period
(probably about 3 months).

OTHER INFORMATION: lifespan up to
13 years in captivity. Solitary, but
sometimes hunted in pairs or small
family groups.

CONSERVATION STATUS: probably
became extinct in 1933. Apart from loss
of habitat to settlers and competition
with introduced dogs, it was relentlessly
persecuted for killing sheep.

NUMBAT

Myrmecobius fasciatus

Banded anteater, Marsupial anteater
Family: Myrmecobiidae

THE NUMBAT IS THE ONLY TRULY DAY-ACTIVE
*Australian marsupial. It feeds almost exclu-
sively on ants and termites; it can eat up to
20,000 termites each day, licking them up
with its long tongue.*

DISTRIBUTION: dry open forests and
scrub of the extreme southwest of
Australia.

SIZE: HB 175–275 mm (6.8–10.7 in);
TL 130–170 mm (5.1–6.6 in);
SH 800 mm (31.2 in); WT 275–550 g
(9.7–19.4 oz).

FORM: color grayish-brown to brick
red, with whitish underparts; there are
6–9 white bars between the mid-back
and the base of the tail, giving a striped
appearance.

DIET: ants and termites.

BREEDING: 2–4 young born at a time.

OTHER INFORMATION: lifespan at least
6 years in captivity.

CONSERVATION STATUS: endangered;
already extinct in New South Wales and
South Australia, mainly as a result of
destruction of its habitat for agriculture, burning of habitat for pasture
and introduced predators.

MARSUPIAL MOLE

Notoryctes typhlops

Family: Notoryctidae

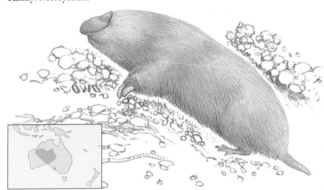

DISTRIBUTION: deserts and semi-deserts of Australia, in northern and east-central Western Australia, southern Northern Territory, and western South Australia.

SIZE: HB 90–180 mm (3.5–7.0 in); TL 12–26 mm (0.5–1 in); WT 40–70 g (1.4–2.5 oz).

FORM: color grayish to golden-yellow or reddish, with whitish underparts. Tail short and naked. Limbs short, strong and stubby, with two large, flat digging claws on each forefoot. Blind; has vestigial eyes 1 mm across, hidden under skin. External ears absent. Pouch of female opens to rear, so as not to fill with earth when burrowing.

THE MARSUPIAL MOLE IS THE ONLY MOLE-LIKE *marsupial. It "swims" just below the surface when foraging, sending up low ridges of sand. However, it burrows down to 2.5 m (8.2 ft) or more to make a permanent home and nursery.*

DIET: insect larvae, especially those of beetles and moths.

BREEDING: 1–2 young born at a time.

OTHER INFORMATION: lifespan 1.5 years. Snout has a horny nasal plate, which it uses to push through the soil. The neck vertebrae are fused for extra rigidity. Both hindlimbs and tail are used to remove soil.

CONSERVATION STATUS: not at risk.

SPOTTED CUSCUS

Spilocuscus (Phalanger) maculatus

Family: Phalangeridae

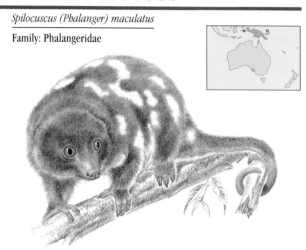

DISTRIBUTION: rainforests, mangroves and open forests of the Cape York Peninsula of Queensland, Australia, and of New Guinea, the Bismarck Archipelago, Ceram and nearby islands.

SIZE: HB 338–442 mm (13.2–17.2 in); TL 315–430 mm (12.3–16.8 in); WT 3–6 kg (6.6–13.2 lb).

FORM: color: males have a spotted pattern of gray and white or brown and white, with a white belly; females are white or gray, often not spotted. Feet have ridged soles for extra grip. Front feet also have sharp claws for climbing. Hind feet have opposable first digits for grasping branches.

THE SPOTTED CUSCUS LIVES HIGH IN THE RAINFOREST *trees. It feeds mainly at night, spending the day sleeping on a leafy platform. It moves very slowly, curling its naked tail round branches for extra safety.*

DIET: mainly leaves, flowers and fruits; also insects, small vertebrates, eggs.

BREEDING: 1–3 young born at a time, after a gestation of about 13 days.

OTHER INFORMATION: lifespan over 11 years in captivity.

CONSERVATION STATUS: rare in Australia, more common in New Guinea; threatened by hunting, and by loss of its forest habitat.

GRAY CUSCUS

Phalanger orientalis

Family: Phalangeridae

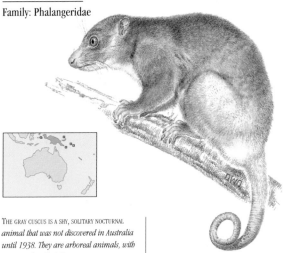

THE GRAY CUSCUS IS A SHY, SOLITARY NOCTURNAL *animal that was not discovered in Australia until 1938. They are arboreal animals, with strong prehensile tails.*

DISTRIBUTION: rainforests of the Moluccas, Ceram, east to New Guinea, the Bismarck Archipelago, Solomon Islands, Louisiade Archipelago, to Cape York in Queensland, Australia.

SIZE: HB 350–550 mm (13.7–21.5 in); TL 280–420 mm (10.9–16.4 in); WT 1.5 –2.2 kg (3.3–4.8 lb).

FORM: grayish-brown, sometimes with a darker stripe along midline of back; underparts whitish. Males sometimes all-white. Tail naked and prehensile. Thin yellow rim around eyes.

DIET: leaves, buds, flowers, fruits.

BREEDING: 1–3 young born at a time, after a gestation of about 13 days; Usually one or two young are suckled.

OTHER INFORMATION: rests by day in a hollow tree. Cuscuses are slow moving and sluggish, resembling the Slow loris of Asia in their movements.

CONSERVATION STATUS: threatened by loss of its forest habitat, and by hunting for its meat. In Australia, it is now rare as a result of logging and mining.

COMMON BRUSH-TAIL POSSUM

Trichosurus vulpecula

Family: Phalangeridae

DISTRIBUTION: throughout Australia, in most habitats, including urban areas. Introduced to New Zealand for the fur market.

SIZE: HB 320–580 mm (12.5–22.6 in); TL 240–350 mm (9.4–13.7 in); WT 1.3–5.0 kg (2.9–11 lb).

FORM: color extremely variable, with four main color phases: gray, brown, black-and-white and cream. Males often have reddish shoulders.

DIET: leaves, shoots, flowers, fruits, seeds; also insects.

BREEDING: only one young born at a time, after a gestation of 15–18 days. Sometimes breeds twice a year.

OTHER INFORMATION: lifespan up to 7 years. An aggressive fighter. If disturbed, it makes a clicking sound.

THE COMMON BRUSH-TAIL POSSUM IS A SOLITARY *animal, advertising its territory and its social status to other animals with a wide range of scents, secreted by at least nine different glands. It also uses loud screeches, hisses, grunts and growls to warn off rivals.*

If seriously threatened, it rears up on its hind legs, stretching out its arms, and screams. A serious pest in some areas, damaging plantations and crops. Shelters in the old nests and burrows.

CONSERVATION STATUS: not at risk.

GREATER GLIDER

Petauroides volans

Greater gliding possum
Family: Petauridae

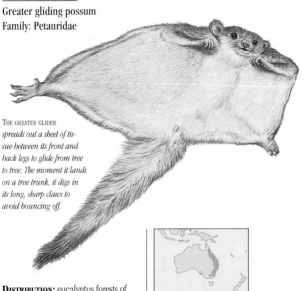

THE GREATER GLIDER
spreads out a sheet of tissue between its front and back legs to glide from tree to tree. The moment it lands on a tree trunk, it digs in its long, sharp claws to avoid bouncing off.

DISTRIBUTION: eucalyptus forests of coastal Australia, from Queensland to southern Victoria.

SIZE: HB 350–450 mm (13.7–17.6 in); TL 450–600 mm (17.6–23.4 in); WT 0.9 –1.7 kg (2–3.7 lb).

FORM: color ranges from creamy-white to smoky-gray or black, with white to dark gray or black underparts. Unlike true gliders, the flight membrane starts at the elbow, not at the fingers. Tail long and prehensile, evenly furred.

DIET: eucalyptus leaves. Has a large cecum containing symbiotic bacteria to help it digest the tough plant material.

BREEDING: one young born at a time, after an unknown gestation period.

OTHER INFORMATION: lifespan about 15 years. Can glide between trees 110 m (361 ft) or more apart.

CONSERVATION STATUS: not at risk.

193

COMMON RINGTAIL POSSUM

Pseudocheirus peregrinus

Family: Petauridae

DISTRIBUTION: dense forests and gardens of Australia, from southern Western Australia and southeastern South Australia to Tasmania and eastern Queensland.

SIZE: HB 300–350 mm (11.7–13.7 in); TL 325–395 mm (12.7–15.4 in); WT 0.7–1.1 kg (1.5–2.4 lb).

FORM: color grayish-brown, darker around the eyes, with whitish underparts; tail dark brown to black, with longish white tip.

DIET: leaves, buds, flowers and fruits. It has a very long cecum containing symbiotic bacteria to help break down tough eucalyptus leaves. It also eats its feces, so that the undigested plant material has a second chance of digestion.

BREEDING: 1–3 young born at a time, after an unknown gestation period; sometimes breeds twice a year.

THE COMMON RINGTAIL POSSUM *gets its name from the pale, curling tip of its tail, which it curls around branches when climbing. It can hang freely from its tail, and climb back up it to get back to the branch.*

OTHER INFORMATION: lifespan up to 6 years in the wild, 8 in captivity. Mainly nocturnal. Shelters by day in a hollow tree or in a large, dome-shaped nest of leaves, which it shares with one or two other possums.

CONSERVATION STATUS: not at risk, but numbers are declining.

FEATHERTAIL POSSUM

Distoechurus pennatus

Pen-tailed possum
Family: Burramyidae

DISTRIBUTION: in small trees and undergrowth of rainforests and moss forests of New Guinea, up to 1,900 m (6,236 ft).

SIZE: HB 100–120 mm (3.9–4.7 in); TL 123–155 mm (4.8–6 in); WT 50–53 g (1.8–1.9 oz).

FORM: color dark brown, with white underparts; face white with black markings around eyes. Tail has two rows of hairs.

DIET: insects and other invertebrates, nectar, pollen, fruits.

BREEDING: 1–2 young born at a time, after an unknown gestation period.

THIS MOUSE-SIZED NOCTURNAL POSSUM HAS TWO *rows of hairs on its tail, which give it a feather-like appearance. A narrow membrane stretched between the elbows and the knees allow the possum to glide for up to 20 m (66 ft).*

OTHER INFORMATION: upper surface of tongue is rough and horny, which is probably used to scrape out the soft flesh of fruits or the insides of insects. Makes nests of leaves in tree hollows, and even in the switch boxes of telephone poles and the pockets of scarecrows.

CONSERVATION STATUS: not known; not thought to be at risk.

195

MOUNTAIN PYGMY POSSUM

Burramys parvus

Family: Burramyidae

DISCOVERED ONLY IN 1966 IN *the kitchen of a ski hut on Australia's highest mountain, the Mountain pygmy possum lives in cold alpine climates, and is the only marsupial known to store caches of food for the winter. It hibernates during the worst weather.*

DISTRIBUTION: subalpine zone of mountains of Australia, between 1,500 and 1,800 m (4,923 and 5,908 ft) in eastern Victoria and the extreme southeast of New South Wales.

SIZE: HB 101–130 mm (3.9–5.1 in); TL 131–160 mm (5.1–6.2 in); WT 30 –60 g (1.1–2.1 oz).

FORM: color grayish-brown to brown, darker toward midline of back and on top of head; underparts paler, usually yellowish-cream or pale brown. Tail covered in hairs so fine that it appears to be naked. Has very large premolars with vertical grooves and serrated cutting edges.

DIET: worms, insects and other invertebrates; seeds, fruits.

BREEDING: 1–4 young born at a time, after a gestation of 13–16 days.

OTHER INFORMATION: lifespan up to 4 years in the wild, 7 in captivity.

CONSERVATION STATUS: endangered, particularly due to habitat loss for the skiing industry.

KOALA

Phascolarctos cinereus

Native bear
Family: Phascolarctidae

THE KOALA IS ABLE TO LIVE ON A *low-nutrient diet of tough eucalyptus leaves because it saves energy by moving very slowly and sleeping almost 18 hours a day.*

DISTRIBUTION: eucalyptus woodlands and forests of Australia, from southeastern Queensland to southeastern South Australia.

SIZE: HB 600–860 mm (23.4–33.5 in); no visible tail; WT 4–15 kg (8.8–33 lb).

FORM: color silvery-gray to reddish-brown, with white underparts; hindquarters often darker brown, sometimes dappled; ears edged with white. Nose large and shiny black. Fur dense and wooly. Has characteristic smell of eucalyptus.

DIET: leaves of certain species of eucalyptus. Has the longest cecum of any mammal, housing bacteria that help digest its food.

BREEDING: one young born at a time, rarely twins, after 34–36 days gestation.

OTHER INFORMATION: lifespan up to 13 years in the wild, 19 in captivity.

CONSERVATION STATUS: decimated by hunting for its fur early in the twentieth century, leaving only scattered populations, now at risk from forest fires.

COMMON WOMBAT

Vombatus ursinus

Coarse-haired, Naked-nosed,
Island, Tasmanian,
Forest wombat
Family: Vombatidae

THE COMMON WOMBAT HAS SHORT, MUSCULAR LEGS *and powerful claws for digging up roots and other plant foods. Colonies of wombats live together in a warren of tunnels, each up to 20 m (64 ft) long, with special sleeping chambers.*

DISTRIBUTION: wet forests of south-eastern Australia, from southeastern Queensland to Tasmania, excluding the Bass Strait islands (where extinct), except Flinders Island.

SIZE: HB 0.7–1.2 m (2.3–3.9 ft); TL about 225 mm (8.8 in); WT 15–39 kg (33–86 lb).

FORM: color ranges from buffish-white to yellowish, silvery-gray, brown, dark brown or black. Hair coarse. Nose round and hairless. Has two rootless incisor teeth in each jaw, as in rodents. Pouch opens backward.

DIET: grasses, herbs, shoots, roots, mushrooms. As in rodents, the teeth grow continuously to make up for the wear caused by tough plant fibers.

BREEDING: only one young born at a time, rarely twins, after a gestation of about 20 days.

OTHER INFORMATION: lifespan over 26 years in captivity.

CONSERVATION STATUS: not at risk, but numbers have declined, especially during the 19th century, as a result of human persecution.

HONEY POSSUM

Tarsipes spenserae

Family: Tarsipedidae

THE HONEY POSSUM IS A SPECIALIST NECTAR-
*feeder and pollinator of Australia's
beathland flowers. Its long snout is
ideal for probing deep into flowers,
and it laps up the nectar with a
long, bristly tongue.*

DISTRIBUTION: tree and
shrub heaths of southwestern
Western Australia.

SIZE: HB 70–85 mm (2.7–3.3 in);
TL 88–100 mm (3.4–3.9 in); WT 7–
12 g (0.25–0.42 oz); female larger
than male.

FORM: color grayish-brown with three
dark stripes along back, the central one
extending to the tail; middle stripes
may be almost black, the outer ones
sometimes reddish-brown; underparts
yellowish-white; limbs reddish-brown.

DIET: mainly nectar, pollen and fruits.
Special hard ridges on its palate help
scrape nectar and pollen off its tongue.

BREEDING: 2–4 young born at a time,
after a gestation of 20–28 days. May
breed up to 4 times a year. Has the
largest sperm of any mammal.

OTHER INFORMATION: lifespan over
1 year. Often huddle together to save
energy; become torpid in cold.

CONSERVATION STATUS: not at risk but
its restricted distribution makes it vulnerable, as its heathland habitat is
destroyed by the spread of urbanization.

QUOKKA

Setonix brachyurus

Family: Macropodidae

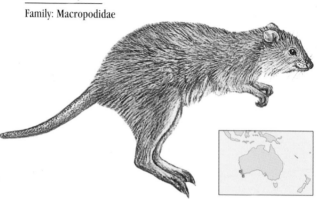

DISTRIBUTION: a few scattered populations in swamps in dry forests of the mainland of southwestern Australia, and dry places on offshore Rottnest and Black Islands.

SIZE: HB 475–600 mm (18.5–23.4 in); TL 250–350 mm (9.75–13.7 in); WT 2–5 kg (4.4–11 lb).

FORM: color brownish-gray, sometimes with a reddish tinge. Tail is only sparsely furred. Ears are short and rounded. Face lacks definite markings.

DIET: grasses and various other plants. Like sheep, it has a special stomach in which bacterial digestion of the plant material takes place.

THE QUOKKA IS A SMALL WALLABY WITH A SHORT *tapering tail. Although it feeds mainly on the ground it can climb small bushes. It is active mainly at night, spending the day sheltering in dense vegetation.*

BREEDING: only one young at a time, in March and April, after a gestation of 24–27 days.

OTHER INFORMATION: lifespan over 10 years. Lives in family groups. Rottnest ("rat nest") Island was originally named after the quokkas, which sailors mistook for rats.

CONSERVATION STATUS: at risk because of its fragmented distribution. The Rottnest Island population is threatened by increased tourism.

BRIDLED NAILTAIL WALLABY

Onychogalea fraenata

Flashjack, Merrin
Family: Macropodidae

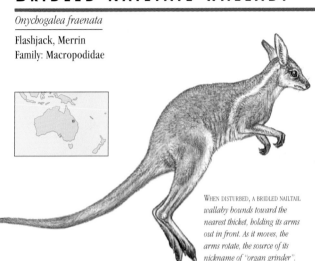

WHEN DISTURBED, A BRIDLED NAILTAIL *wallaby bounds toward the nearest thicket, holding its arms out in front. As it moves, the arms rotate, the source of its nickname of "organ grinder".*

DISTRIBUTION: originally pine and brigalow forests of Australia west of the Great Divide. Now confined to a small area in eastern Queensland.

SIZE: HB 430–700 mm (16.9–27.6 in); TL 360–730 mm (14.2–28.7 in); WT 4–9 kg (8.8–19.8 lb).

FORM: color grayish, with white underparts; white shoulder stripes run from base of ears along back of neck and down back of each shoulder to white underparts.

DIET: roots of grasses and herbs.

BREEDING: only one young born at a time, in May, after an unknown gestation period.

OTHER INFORMATION: lifespan over 7 years in captivity. Nailtail wallabies are shy and usually solitary.

CONSERVATION STATUS: endangered. Once thought to be extinct, as a result of loss of habitat and removal of cover for agriculture and pasture, and predation by introduced dogs and foxes. Rediscovered in 1973 in a small area of central Queensland, part of which is now a reserve.

EASTERN GRAY KANGAROO

Macropus giganteus

Family: Macropodidae

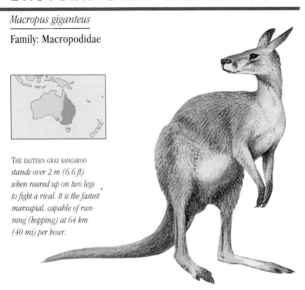

THE EASTERN GRAY KANGAROO *stands over 2 m (6.6 ft) when reared up on two legs to fight a rival. It is the fastest marsupial, capable of running (hopping) at 64 km (40 mi) per hour.*

DISTRIBUTION: grasslands close to forest and woodland in Australia, from eastern and central Queensland to New South Wales, Victoria, southeastern South Australia, and Tasmania.

SIZE: HB 0.5–1.4 m (1.6–4.6 ft); TL 0.4 –1.1 m (1.3–3.6 ft); WT 27.5–54 kg (61–119 lb); male considerably larger than female.

FORM: color silvery-gray, with paler paws. Fur thick and coarse.

DIET: mainly grasses.

BREEDING: only one young born at a time, between September and March, after a gestation of 36–37 days.

OTHER INFORMATION: lifespan up to 20 years. Lives in small temporary groups or "mobs" of up to 10 individuals or more. These are usually females and young, but males join them to breed.

CONSERVATION STATUS: not at risk. Has actually benefited from the spread of human settlements, as the felling of forests and clearing of scrub have produced new pastures for it.

RED KANGAROO

Macropus rufus

Family: Macropodidae

THE RED KANGAROO CAN LEAP A *distance of 12.8 m (42 ft), a record for a marsupial. It may travel up to 300 km (186 mi) across the desert in search of food or water.*

DISTRIBUTION: dry grasslands throughout Australia, except in the extreme north, the east coast and the extreme southwest.

SIZE: HB 0.75–1.4 m (2.5–3.6 ft); TL 0.65–1 m (2.1–3.3 ft); WT 17–85 kg (37–187 lb); male much larger than female.

FORM: color bluish-gray to reddish, with a white belly. The tail gives balance and acts as rudder when leaping.

DIET: grasses and herbs.

BREEDING: only one young born at a time, after a gestation of 33 days.

OTHER INFORMATION: lifespan up to 20 years. The thick fur is an adaptation to desert conditions, insulating it from the heat of the sun. The inner side of the forearms have very little fur. When hot, the kangaroo licks these, and sometimes also its chest, so that the evaporating saliva cools the blood passing through vessels close to the skin. It may also pant to cool itself.

CONSERVATION STATUS: not at risk.

LUMHOLTZ'S TREE KANGAROO

Dendrolagus lumholtzi

Family: Macropodidae

DISTRIBUTION: rainforests of northeastern Queensland, Australia.

SIZE: HB 480–590 mm (18.7–23 in); TL 600–740 mm (23.4–28.9 in); WT 5–10 kg (11–22 lb); male larger than female.

FORM: color mottled grayish to blackish-brown, sometimes greenish-buff, with paler flanks and whitish underparts; feet blackish. Tail long, used as a support when climbing. Feet have roughened soles for gripping tree trunks.

DIET: mainly plants, especially leaves, shoots and fruits.

BREEDING: only one young born at a time, after a gestation of about 32 days.

LUMHOLTZ'S TREE KANGAROO LIVES IN *the Queensland rainforest. It is an agile climber, aided by its strong claws; it can leap 9 m (30 ft) or more from tree to tree, using its tail as a balancer. On the ground it leaps along, arching its tail.*

OTHER INFORMATION: tree kangaroos use their hands in many ways while climbing and are good at manipulating their food. The first and second fingers can be opposed to the other fingers and the forepaws can bend at the wrist.

CONSERVATION STATUS: threatened.

BANDED HARE-WALLABY

Lagostrophus fasciatus

Family: Macropodidae

DISTRIBUTION: extremely rare in southern and southwestern Australia; main populations are found in dense acacia scrub on some islands off the coast of Western Australia.

SIZE: HB 400–460 mm (15.6–17.9 in); TL 320–400 mm (12.5–15.6 in); WT 1.3–3 kg (2.9–6.6 lb).

FORM: color grayish, with transverse light bands across back and upper flanks; underparts buffish-white. Fur is thick, soft and long.

DIET: grasses and herbs. Makes tunnels through dense vegetation from its daytime refuges in acacia thickets to its feeding grounds.

BREEDING: only one young born at a time, rarely twins.

OTHER INFORMATION: lifespan at least 4 years.

CONSERVATION STATUS: endangered. Only small, scattered populations remain, mostly on offshore islands. Main cause of decline is probably competition with sheep and degradation of its feeding grounds by livestock; also predation by introduced foxes.

INDEX